Communicating Reality Through Symbols

Westminster Studies in Christian Communication

Kendig Brubaker Cully, General Editor

Communicating Reality Through Symbols

EVERETT M. STOWE

THE WESTMINSTER PRESS
Philadelphia

LIBRARY OF CONGRESS CATALOG CARD NO. 66-18509

Published by The Westminster Press®
Philadelphia, Pennsylvania

PRINTED IN THE UNITED STATES OF AMERICA

Contents

A Note on Westminster Studies in Christian Communication

These Studies are predicated on the ground that the Christian faith needs to be made relevant to persons in the modern world in terms of the dynamic nature of the faith itself and the channels that are capable of conveying such a faith. In itself any technique of communication conceivably could serve as well for secular as for religious ends. In this series a wide variety of means and methods of communication will be analyzed in the light of their availability to, and suitability for, the particular tasks that the Christian church faces in bringing the realities of faith to bear upon the life of actual persons in the contemporary situation.

Oftentimes in the past, techniques have been viewed almost as ends in themselves. Or, they have been taken over uncritically from the secular culture without being subjected to adequate scrutiny as to whether they are appropriate for the church's use. On the other hand, sometimes the church has been blind to the life situations of the present to such an extent as to ignore the real ways in which people's lives are influenced by all that impinges on them. In the latter case, the church has failed to bring the life-giving power of the gospel to bear on contemporary culture because of a lack of understanding of, or appreciation for, the means of communication that have been proved capable of changing lives and societies.

Involving as it does both the "What" and the "How," the whole question of the communication of the gospel in the modern world is pivotal in the present juncture of history. The present Studies will be aimed at bringing the "What" and the "How" together fruitfully. These books are designed to make a contribution to the ongoing conversations across boundaries. Theology, Biblical studies, sociology, cultural anthropology, psychology, education, art, letters, science and the other disciplines, all have something to say to one another. In our present concern, " communication " refers to the way in which the Christian faith can come into conjunction with what is happening in the total world of life and ideas in the middle decades of the twentieth century. In each of these Studies attention will focus on some important aspect of the basic question: How can the church most effectively preach, teach, and otherwise manifest the gospel in the growing edges of man's present-day culture? No aspect of man's actual situation is alien to such a question. No medium of communication should fail to come under scrutiny if, as Christians, we are eager to have the Word of God confront a confused generation powerfully and compellingly.

Each volume in Westminster Studies in Christian Communication will be an authentic voice of one perceptive interpreter. No effort has been made to suggest to any writer what " line " he ought to follow. Each work will be adjudged by the readers on its own merits. The writers themselves conceivably might disagree heartily with regard to certain presuppositions or conclusions held by their colleagues. All this will be to the good if the result of these Studies should be the stimulating of many conversations. Yet all the writers have in mind a focus that is realistic, an emphasis that is practical, and a discussion that is timely. The only request made of the authors is that they speak out of their knowledge to the very heart and mind of our times. Depth without dullness, breadth without diffuseness, challenge without sentimentality – these, at least, it is hoped, will be characteristic of all the Studies. We are grateful to those who have consented to share in this venture into communication, and we commend their work as in itself an integral part of the church's task of communication.

KENDIG BRUBAKER CULLY
General Editor

New York City

Preface

A child at the conclusion of an entrancing story is likely to ask: "Is it true? Did it really happen?" While fantasy has its own satisfactions for the thirsting imagination, there is also in the questing mind an insatiable hunger for the truly real.

In the first of his *Four Quartets,* T. S. Eliot reminds us that humankind cannot bear very much reality. Yet this is an age in which no one can evade encounter with fresh realities. Man in his recent history has had to think the unthinkable in his confrontation with newly understood dimensions of space and time, the interchangeability of energy and mass, the possible cataclysms of history. These and other concerns have been added to the attempt to know himself and to penetrate farther into the mysteries of reality. The human spirit stands at the threshold of an epoch that promises to be unique in its threatening demands and in its untold possibilities.

In man's search for what is real he has had recourse to symbols. An image or word or act is symbolic when it intends more than it says, when it implies more than its immediate meaning. So attractive is this capacity that symbolizing may run wild. There is ground for the assertion of Alfred North Whitehead that "the life of humanity can easily be overwhelmed by its symbolic accessories." Yet this thinker immediately adds that nature, expelled with a pitchfork, ever returns, and men have to find symbols in order to express themselves.

The meanings of symbolization have been given intensive attention within recent years by thinkers and workers in varied fields — artists, scientists, philosophers, theologians, linguists, and students of culture and of depth psychology. Despite the wide variety of approaches, a central theme is furnished by the human capacity for symbolic transformation. Symbolizing has been characterized as the generative idea of a coming age.

The term " reality " is used with due caution by a generation that has undergone radical changes of outlook. So drastic and heterogeneous have these changes been that existence may come to seem absurd. This outlook is expressed in the theater of the absurd and in novels and other works of literature. An influential stream of thought in India, centered on *maya,* considers the flow of time as we experience it to be a form of cosmic illusion. Further, there are paradoxes in science that raise the question as to whether nature reflects meaningful order, and incongruities in culture that contribute to the ironies of history. These and other aspects of life and thought in this era give special point to a study of symbolic forms. If they suggest images of reality, it is to be remembered that the image has its own reality.

E. M. S.

New York City

Chapter I

The Symbol: Organ of the Human

The images that are given through physical sight foreshadow in man his unique capacities for imaginative insight and for symbolizing activities.

In response to the given reality of light, some living cells developed sensitivity in remote times. Through the course of ages these light-sensitive cells have become part of the tissues of the delicately complex structure of the eye. Physical sight meant myriad mutual relationships between flowering plants and insect and bird pollinators, and groupings sprang up that were knit by visual as well as chemical signals. This fact has led to the assertion that "life is thus ultimately a photo-chemical phenomenon." [1]

Human capacities for physical sight have been enormously extended and enlarged through the telescope and the microscope. Through the largest telescope, for instance, can be faintly discerned the object catalogued by astronomers as 3C-286, as far distant, perhaps, as seven to ten billion light-years. The electron microscope reveals a no less remarkable reality in making visible what seems to our perceptions almost infinitely small. The facts of sight substantiate this observation of Pierre Teilhard de Chardin: "The history of the living world can be summarised as the elaboration of ever more perfect eyes within a cosmos in which there is always something more to be seen." [2] He characterizes this capacity for sight as a mysterious gift of existence.

Within the human self, vision is of more than what is "out there." Within the self there is a transforming capacity for imagination and understanding. Meister Eckhardt observed that, if we subtract the mind, the eye is open to no purpose. Artists of the Orient learned centuries ago that the perfection of depicting plant or bird depended on steeping oneself, perhaps for months, in the true appearance until it became indelibly a part of the inner being of the artist.

The differentiation between animal reaction and human response inheres in the capacity of man to transform into meaning the images that come through sight or other senses. The mind is not merely a switchboard for sorting out the signals that come to it; rather, it is a "transformer," as Susanne Langer has pointed out. If the history of the living world is indeed marked by the elaboration of ever more perfect eyes, the basic fact of the human world is the power of symbolic transformation of outward images and the imaginative construction of inward images.

On one occasion an immigrant accompanied by his pet dog was observed on the deck of a steamer approaching the Statue of Liberty in New York Harbor. Tears were silently coursing down the deeply lined face of the newcomer as his eyes fell for the first time on that emblem of freedom. But the pet animal, however gifted with acute eyesight, could not *see* that uplifted torch. Or suppose a seabird swooping from a height for a tidbit of food – contrast its image with that of Emma Lazarus, whose poem, rich in metaphors, is inscribed at the base of the monument:

> Give me your tired, your poor,
> Your huddled masses yearning to breathe free,
> The wretched refuse of your teeming shore.
> Send these, the homeless, tempest-tost to me,
> I lift my lamp beside the golden door.

In man, what is seen is seen through the eyes with the mind. The sensuous and the intelligible are formed into a constructive whole. The form and the matter of perception are linked through conceptual thinking and pictorial imaging in the interpretation by the self of what is perceived. There is little point in arguing which element is the more important. The mind and the eye are inextricably involved in the formation of perceptual judgments, and as Thomas Aquinas noted, "Vision is made actual only when the thing seen is in a certain way in the seer."

This fundamental characteristic of the mind — the active and constitutive seizing on and molding what the senses bring — was pointed out by the philosopher Immanuel Kant (1724–1804). He observed that experience is, without doubt, the first product of our understanding. The moth dances to its death about the flame; no amount of painful singeing means experience. Persons with severely retarded minds may repeat processes endlessly without learning. For them, the bases for experience from understanding are not present. Such persons often are not able to carry out a simple symbolic act, such as assuming to drink a glass of water unless water is actually there.

In the normal mind, however, so Kant said, there are inborn structures and functions that transform the stream of images into meaning. These constitutive capacities and activities are the very ground for being a self. Kant characterized his discovery of the constructive activity within the mind as a "Copernican revolution." As the astronomer Copernicus made clear that the planets of our solar system revolve about the sun as their common center, so Kant found the center of thought to be the regulative principles of the mind whose categories provide a framework for its functioning.

His Copernican revolution has been a profound and continuing one, both through later thinkers who disagree and through others who modify but build upon Kantian thought. One of the recent thinkers who seized on Kant's insights to broaden and expand them was Ernst Cassirer (1874–1945). He acknowledged a deep and continuing debt to Kant's contribution, but he enlarged the dimensions of those contributions.

The central fact of human existence, Cassirer asserted, is

man's capacity to respond to symbols. The ability to effect a symbolic transformation of images is the central clue to what is most significantly human, and the clue also to man's closest apprehension of reality. In Cassirer's *The Philosophy of Symbolic Forms* (three volumes written in the 1920's) is to be found his exhaustive study of certain symbolic forms. In *An Essay on Man* (1944), Cassirer underscores and extends the centrality of symbolic forms as the clue to the human. His many other writings bear on this central conviction in one way or another.

Consider some of the varieties of symbolic forms:

Mythical thought is of almost universal occurrence as men, whether archaic or modern, weave into symbolic narrative their responses to cosmic processes or to the great facts of their existence. Mythical thought is well-nigh universal and persists as part of the indelible mental furnishings of finite beings.

Language is symbolic expression and is a mark of humanity as universal as mankind himself. However diverse in forms, it has unity of symbolic function.

Art is as integral to human existence as is mythical thought and language. Mankind's very earliest records testify to the form-giving impulse for artistic expression. This impulse is no less powerful now than when it led, perhaps twenty thousand years ago, to the superb paintings in caves in what are now France and Spain and other countries.

Religion in its manifold forms is permeated with symbolic expression. Religious symbols take on a distinctive quality which reflects man's response to the *mysterium tremendum*, to the holy, to the sacred, to all he associates with his gods, or with God as the ground of all existence.

Science, a dominant fact in our era, is popularly supposed to deal with hard fact and the finality of sense data. Yet in current understandings of science there is seen to be an indispensable recognition of symbolism and its functions.

Present-day living confronts man with a flood of images. Many can be viewed under one or another of the symbolic forms noted above. What is of central significance for man as the *animal symbolicum* is the process of constructive activity within man as he encounters and molds these symbolic forms. To use Cassirer's own words:

> Man has, as it were, discovered a new method of adapting himself to his environment. Between the receptor system and the effector system, which are to be found in all animal species, we find in man a third link which we may describe as the *symbolic system*. This new acquisition transforms the whole of human life. As compared with the other animals man lives not merely in a broader reality; he lives, so to speak, in a new *dimension* of reality.[3]

The key fact for this insight is that human response to existence is constructive, not passive. "Seeing is translating" rather than "seeing is believing." This generative idea is the philosophical theme of the coming age, in the view of those who see in symbolic transformation the organ of what is distinctively human.

To assert this significance of symbolic forms is not to discount sense data. We have this treasure in earthen vessels. This was pointed out by Kant himself, who said that the dove winging through the air and feeling its resistance might suppose airless flight easier, forgetting that the very air was its support. So with sense impression. "Ideas are undoubtedly made out of impressions," states Susanne Langer, adding that these sense messages come from the organs of perception and vague visceral reports of feeling. These materials brought by the senses, however, are constantly wrought into symbols. Further, "the fact that the human brain is constantly carrying on a process of symbolic transformation of the experiential data that come to it causes it to be a veritable fountain of more or less spontaneous ideas."[4]

What flows together in the symbol is the sensuous and the intelligible, the image and the meaning. As physical sight is light-needing, so the human understanding and spirit are image-needing, used symbolically to disclose what is beyond them. Cassirer's own words are that it is through these image worlds alone " that we see what we call ' reality ' and in them alone we possess it: for the highest objective truth that is accessible to the spirit is ultimately the form of its own activity." [5]

Another Dimension of the Symbol

If symbolic forms are basic for discursive reason, they are no less so for the depths of the self below the level of the conscious. It is a curious and significant fact that the term which is a unique key for philosophy in the study of ways of knowing is equally central for the depths of the unconscious.

In literature, and through dreams, the existence of the world of the unconscious was surmised long millennia before the work of such men as Freud, Jung, Adler, Rank, and others. The Chinese sage Chuang-tze, in the fourth century B.C., put in these words his recognition of realities of being which are below the level of the conscious: " Last night I dreamed that I was a butterfly, and now I do not know whether I am a man who dreamt that he was a butterfly, or a butterfly which now dreams it is a man." In Greece the dramas of Sophocles that centered on Oedipus gave form to deep-lying tensions in family relationships, which have been analyzed by depth psychology more than two thousand years after they were given symbolic expression in the mythology and the drama of Greece. The power of such great poetic drama is as alive today as is the form of a Greek vase or a torso by the sculptor Phidias. Gilbert Murray in a comment on the dramas of Greece refers to the ways they speak to " an under-current of desires and fears and passions, long slumbering yet eternally familiar, which have for thousands of years lain near the root of our most intimate emotions and been wrought into the fabric of our most magical dreams."

The novel *Moby Dick,* by Herman Melville (1819–1891), shows the flame of a lamp used to illuminate the forces at work within the crew members who are setting out on the rolling sea to search for the great white whale that had maimed the body of Captain Ahab. The novel can be read on one level as an entrancing story. On quite another, and deeper, level it reveals powerful forces at work within the human spirit, set forth in unforgettable metaphors that go to depths other than discursive reason alone. Just before setting sail the crew hears the sermon by Father Mapple on Jonah. That prophet is portrayed as appalled by his conscience as he looks on the lamp in his ship's cabin. Noting the steadiness of the flame despite the vessel's heaving motion, Jonah exclaims: " Oh, so my conscience hangs in me! Straight upward so it burns, but the chambers of my soul are all in crookedness." But with the revenge-driven captain of the *Pequod*, it is quite otherwise. Captain Ahab calls his crew, who range from primitive island men to the matter-of-fact Starbuck, to join in binding oaths to hunt the white whale to the death. He exclaims, " And that ye may know to what tune this heart beats, look ye here while I thus blow out the last fear! " And with one mighty blast he extinguishes the flame, and the fateful voyage is on over the heaving sea that no human effort can permanently mark.

As Kant's Copernican revolution led to deepened insight on symbolic forms as constructive expressions of the conscious self, so insights from depth psychology have helped modern man become aware of an unsuspected heritage of patterns of impulse and partially hidden thought. These archetypal patterns, to use a favorite term of Carl G. Jung, are not static forms. Rather, they mark a dynamic process. Jung asserted that: " The content of a symbol can never be fully expressed in rational terms. It stems from the intermediate realm of subtle reality which can only be adequately expressed by the symbol." [6] Jung goes on to say that it is the true apprehension of the power of the symbol that marks the difference between culture and civilization. An interpreter of Jung says: " For civilization is always a child of the *ratio*, the intellect; culture, however, grows from the spirit, and spirit is never wholly confined to the consciousness like the intellect, but also encompasses, masters, and gives form to all the depths of the unconscious, of primordial nature." [7]

Students of depth psychology discover persisting psychobiological characteristics that transcend cultural boundaries. Thus there is a kinship as to the nature of dreams. Dreams have been characterized as the one universal language that the human race has ever developed. They confirm the fact that what is called the *psyche* has areas that are not identical with consciousness. Susanne Langer makes this observation:

> Only certain products of the symbol-making brain can be used according to the canons of discursive reasoning. In every mind there is an enormous store of other symbolic material, which is put to different uses, or perhaps to no use at all — a mere result of spontaneous brain activity, a reserve fund of conceptions, a surplus of mental wealth.[8]

This " surplus " has two sources — the values of living as understood by the self, and the persistent elemental factors from our psychobiological heritage. This archaic heritage concerns such fundamentals as birth, parent figures, food, sexuality, marriage, and death. The values arise from living experience, now profoundly affected by unprecedented transformations of the social and physical environment. Symbols carry both historical content and emotional significance, as images from one's existence and their meanings are related to relatively universal human impulses.

Symbols come into being at the boundary where the self, with its powers of knowing and of intuition, meets the world. The flourishing of symbolic expression is an index of the urge to see, to *know*. The impulse to symbolic form pervaded archaic life — the dance, meticulous ritual, artistic expression, story and myth, religious symbols in unending profusion, and so on. But the emphasis on the symbol is no less marked in this day. Anthropologists and psychologists have intensively studied symbolism and communication. Philosophers have given searching thought to symbol and language, as have literary artists from their own concern for expression. Symbolic logic relates the rigor of mathematical thinking to legitimate use of language. A. J. Ayer, in his *Language, Truth, and Logic,* flatly asserts that it is impossible for a sentence to be significant and to be about God! Theologians and natural scientists have from their respective viewpoints given large place to symbolism in their disciplines.

These modern studies are added to traditional emphasis on the symbol at a moment in human history when the human being has had to make vast new attempts to understand the realities of a universe that confronts him with deepening mystery. If the symbol affords images of reality, the person of this day wants to know it as he wrestles to achieve sound truth and living faith. If the form of the mind's activity is indeed inseparable from symbolic form, then here is, Cassirer asserts, an indispensable key to the highest objective truth.

Chapter II

Protean Change and Persistent Symbolizing

A story from Martin Buber tells of a pious rabbi, Eisik of Cracow, who dreamed that he should journey to Prague to unearth a treasure buried there next to a bridge. He found the spot, but it was guarded by sentinels, whose captain told the rabbi of a dream of his own – that he, the captain, should go to Cracow to look for a treasure buried in the house of a certain rabbi Eisik. The captain had put no trust in the dream. But the rabbi on returning to his own home did indeed discover the treasure buried there. A comment on this story says:

> Thus the real treasure, that which can put an end to our poverty and all our trials, is never very far; there is no need to seek it in a distant country. It lies buried in the most intimate parts of our own house; that is, of our own being. It is behind the stove, the center of the life and warmth that rule our existence, the heart of our heart, if only we knew how to unearth it.[1]

There is the further comment on this story that it is only after a pious journey to a new land that the meaning of the inner voice guiding our search can make itself understood, perhaps through one who is a stranger and of another belief and race.

The symbols men live by differ as do their languages. But as languages, however diverse in sound and structure, fulfill need and possibility of speech, so do symbols constitute the "heart of our heart," whatever the variety of content.

Our era is one in which contrasting beliefs and different races have been brought into ever closer contacts. Even in the remote past there was a migration of certain symbolic expressions. One of these, for example, is the swastika. It is found in remains of early Aegean and Danubian cultures. It also occurred in places as distant from each other as what is now northern Europe and India, and even farther east. It was a symbol of the four cardinal directions and their deities and was taken over by worshipers of Buddha and of Vishnu. Similarly, there is a widespread occurrence of certain other forms, such as the mandala, spiral, whirlpool, and so on.

It is within the past three centuries that there has occurred the widest encounter of differing cultural systems, each with its characteristic symbolic expressions. An illustration is given by Professor F. S. C. Northrop on the meeting of East and West. He argues that the East has traditionally given primacy to the aesthetic and intuitive approach to reality. Thus a Chinese landscape painting, in blue monochrome of varying shades to convey the sense of distance, in an almost magical way shows the underlying conviction of the presence of the *Tao,* the way, that pervades all things of nature and of man. Now each of these shades of blue can be precisely denoted by its own characteristic wavelength; the physicist can measure them with great exactness. Here are two characteristic approaches to the realities of nature — one by the artist, one by the scientist. This scholar maintains that the meeting of East and West is an encounter of contrasting emphases and of distinctive symbolisms.[2]

The one outlook is chiefly intuitive and synoptic, this argument says, while the other is in the main analytic and intellectual. But whatever may have been true in the early encounter of the symbolisms of East and West, history has seen some modifications taking place. Thus a Chinese emperor at the end of the eighteenth century disclaimed any possible interest in anything that envoys from England's King could conceivably bring to the Middle Kingdom. But that country's government is now host to the outlook of Marx and Lenin (with distinctive Chinese modifications, true), a wholesale adoption of an extreme aspect of a Western interpretation of life.

In the mid-nineteenth century the black ships of Commodore Perry appeared off the coast of Japan. The doors on millennia-old patterns of culture were forced open. In the intervening century, that ancient culture has felt the powerful impact of the heritage of the West. Modern buildings in Japan are now typically in reinforced concrete and in the form of an architectural Esperanto that gives common appearance to such structures wherever they are built. The life of modern Japan is the fascinating scene of the working out of values, and appropriate symbolic expression, of what are held to be living alternatives in the encounter of East and West in that particular setting.

Not only is there the encounter of contemporary cultures. There is the meeting, in our enforced physical unity in a shrinking world, of the archaic and primitive, on the one hand, and the ultrasophisticated patterns of modern disciplines, on the other hand.

There are places where men still live an essentially Stone Age existence. These are found in the deserts of Australia, in the valleys of New Guinea, in the mountains of the high Andes. These Stone Age relics coexist with so-called advanced cultures. The gap between them has one measure, for example, in the elementary capacities in mathematics on the part of these archaic men in contrast to the sophistication of modern computers, whose resources in computation so greatly extend man's intellectual endeavors.

It is true that astonishing adaptations can be made by peoples of primitive traditions under the sudden impact of the techniques and living patterns of the modern world. Studies have been made, in certain island cultures of the Pacific, of communities that in one generation have moved from the very ancient ways of the past into the modern world. It seems likely that the process of swift change in outlook and ways of living will continue with accelerating speed. These protean changes confront primitive and sophisticated men alike with crises of the spirit.

In *An Essay on Man*, Ernst Cassirer concludes his chapter on " Facts and Ideals " with these words: " It is symbolic thought which overcomes the natural inertia of man and endows him with a new ability, the ability constantly to reshape his human universe."[3] He points out that the character of human knowledge is such that it can make a sharp distinction between the reality and the possibility of things. Animals are confined within the world of sense perceptions; they can form no idea of " possible " things. But to man it is possible to have imaginative insight. The physical basis is due in part to a greater cranial capacity, in part to a long infancy of biological helplessness that makes necessary that first cultural grouping, a family, at least of sorts. Whatever the situations confronted by humanity in an epoch of unprecedented change, the persistent capacity for symbolizing activities means reshaping the human universe.

Some Characteristics of Symbols

The very word " symbol " seems alive with meaning. Yet the term is used in so many senses that it may come to lose its unique power. Associated with this term are allied words — " sign," " signal," " metaphor," " icon," " emblem," and others. Clarification of their meanings is required for depth of apprehension of symbolic forms.

The specific term " symbol " has its roots in Greek. The noun *symbolon* was applied to an ancient custom of hospitality of the Greek people. After an occasion of hospitality, a Greek host would give to a departing guest a broken-off half of a ring or coin. The two parts could again be matched on some future occasion. And in the absence of the two friends from each other, the part that each retained would represent graphically the whole experience of entertainment and of continuing friendship.

Another term in Greek that entered into the making of the word " symbol " was *symballein,* meaning " to throw together," or " to bring together." What is brought together in the symbol is not things but conceptions. A sign may be a visible or audible signal. But a symbol is an interpretation by mind or imagination of something that has entered into the field of observation. Goethe said that true symbolism is when the particular represents the general, as a " vivid instantaneous revelation of that which cannot be explored."

In the instance of the Greek custom of the *symbolon,* the part – the broken coin or ring – is taken for a larger whole, and this is a feature of the act of symbolizing. There is no actual connection between the two parts of the object shared by parting host and guest except the conceptions that each has abstracted from the experience. The part means the larger whole.

A related feature of the symbol is its *power.* From the stream of human experience at any given moment, one can identify incidents or acts that manifest the fact of almost irrepressible power. For example: In Kashmir in late 1963, there was stolen from a Mohammedan mosque a relic of the Prophet in the form of a single strand of hair. The incident caused a riot. More than 100,000 Muslims took part in it. Fires were set, shots were fired, and many died in the melee. What power to be channeled through a single, slender thread of hair!

Another incident is from the life of India. The government in 1964 announced an official policy of making Hindi the official language of the country as a whole. In protest a young man in Madras, where the Hindi tongue is almost completely foreign, set fire to himself. His suicide, followed by others for the same cause, was counted on to manifest an unbreakable determination to continue the use of the mother tongue of the people of Madras. Self-incineration made it indelibly clear that this value was counted dearer than life itself.

The power embodied in symbolic expression need not be in the form of external violence. Consider the formidable struggle now quietly taking place in Soviet Russia between artists and government policy. The official insistence has been that all art forms must be for the ends of "socialist realism." To the artist, such a policy, doing violence to the inner image which grasps him in its power, is simply not to be tolerated.

An instance of this struggle is seen in the poetry of Alexander Solzhenitsyn. This man survived eight years in Soviet concentration camps.[4] The vision that sustained him through that experience came to expression in four recent poems.[5] One commentator on these poems notes that in almost every line there is a shift from Soviet realism to symbolism. The poet finds in the bell towers of the churches of Russia, rising above the thatch, reminders of how necessary it is to relinquish an hour to eternity. He ponders how "in these bell towers our forebears placed all that was best of them."

In contemplating this art form and others of present-day Russia, one glimpses in their expression an indestructible reality and an unquenchable thirst for truth that is more fundamental than can be expressed in even the most thoroughgoing forms of socialist realism.

It is in religion that the evidence of the symbol as power is most strikingly evident. In the Boxer uprising in China at the turn of the century, Chinese Christians often were given the choice of treading on a cross as an act of abandonment of their faith or else forfeiting their lives. Great numbers took the way of martyrdom rather than perform that simple piece of ritual. The history of religions is replete with the record of symbolic acts, which show in radical ways the willingness to bring for sacrifice that which most undeniably and fully expresses one's ultimate concern — even of one's firstborn or one's own life.

These instances reflect certain underlying and persistent symbolic forms — the mythic power of a tradition that comes to a burning focus in a relic; the profoundly emotional issues involved in a mother tongue; the irrepressible urge to artistic expression that incarnates an inner vision; the force of an explicit religious faith. Nor is the fact of power absent from science. For, as Michael Polanyi observes, "science, by virtue of its passionate note, finds its place among the great systems of utterances which try to evoke and impose correct modes of feeling. In teaching its own kinds of formal excellence science functions like art, religion, morality, law, and other constituents of culture." [6]

A further feature of the symbol is its relation with "value." A national flag can become an emblem of the participation of its followers in a particular political community. The fierce loyalties generated by loyalty to a flag may have an almost transcendent force. In our era, nationalism has been called man's other religion. There is an elaborate ritual that surrounds the treatment of a national flag. It *participates* in the reality it is meant to represent. Burning or trampling a national flag is an act with its own fiercely symbolic meaning.

A flag may come to stand for a perverted sense of values, of course, as in the case of the *Hakenkreuz* carried by the Nazi followers of Hitler. That the values are perverted may not diminish the symbolic potency of the emblem.

Participation in value is a persistent feature of symbolization. It follows that changing systems of values mean a shifting order of symbolic expression. But this does not mean that there is a diminution of the significance of the persistent symbolic forms which are the organ of the human. Thus in the South Seas, anthropologists have studied the meaning of ceremonial gifts of choice yams that are given, not for mundane food value, but for the relations between tribal or clan or village communities. The onrush of a mechanical order on these societies may cause these traditions to evaporate. But unless there is developed an appropriate form of expression to replace the one outmoded by changed ways of living, that society may rapidly disintegrate. The symbol is not a thing, observes Dorothy D. Lee, but rather, it is a point in a creative process.[7]

But why symbols at all? If they point to reality, why not grasp that reality directly? These queries are natural to a culture where the mechanical supersedes the organic realities.

Ernst Cassirer points out that because of what man is he cannot escape from his own achievement. He must adopt the conditions of his own life. He does not live in a merely physical universe. He lives in a symbolic universe, and language, myth, art, and religion are parts of this universe. These weave a symbolic net so that man deals not with things themselves, but is in constant conversation with himself. There is, thus, all the more reason for a discerning understanding of the symbolic forms that surround his existence, of the richness and variety of cultural life, of the upsurging vitalities of the unconscious depths of his being, adding emotional to conceptual language.

With the predominant concern with natural science in this era, many have been persuaded that symbolisms could be dispensed with as airy figments left over from a mythological past. Some scientists show how much beside the point this is.

Persistence of the Person

The word "person" originated from two Latin words: *per* and *sonare*, meaning literally "to sound through." The foundation for its use was drama. In many theatrical traditions the actors put on masks that typified a given character — the evil one, the trickster, the hero, and so on. The actor spoke through the mask, and his words were those the dramatist gave him. Yet even the external mask could not suppress the fact that it was an individual speaking, and the genius of the great actor "sounded through" in a personal way.

The person in history is influenced by external forces, yet he is not inevitably a helpless creature of those forces. In creative moments there occur special opportunities for the person to manifest his original and distinctive powers. All cultures reveal tendencies to movement, and in these movements, individual and community may become potent forces. One thinks of the influence of Dante in the West, for example — "the voice of ten silent centuries" — whose *Divine Comedy* stirred deeply the peoples who moved into the Renaissance against the background of the elaborate symbolism of the Inferno, Purgatorio, and Paradiso. In other cultures there is to be seen the ebb and flow of forces that are at bottom an intermixture of the realities of the self and of the physical environment provided by nature and by man.

Our era is indeed one of protean change. And there has entered upon the stage of history the widest representation of peoples and cultures. But there are certain typical manifestations of our time that tend to become dominant, particularly in their influence upon personal existence.

There is, for instance, the fact of techniques and of mass order. The chief possibility for making a living is increasingly through technology – through the assembly line. Along with this is the predominance of urban living. The resulting problems lead to enhanced functions of the political state. The most recent stage of technology is the emergence of computer control. It is true that these new means of physical control and rapid computer handling of complicated data may make possible, in a new way, the human use of human beings. The alternative to that is a technological order of robots. The consequences of such an order were portrayed by Charles Chaplin in a notable film, *Modern Times,* displaying sardonic humor and fateful prescience. Whatever the form of development of this infant prodigy in the field of economic production, computer techniques, and the controls of "cybernation" (from the Greek term for "helmsman"), it seems certain that there will be a further extension of human power over the physical world. It was Albert Einstein, commenting on the discovery of nuclear fission and its awesome power (which can be used for the good or ill of humanity), who said that this discovery had changed everything but man's thinking!

A by-product of this technological order is that man tends to become a mere tool, a means to an end. In the typical industrial process he makes but a fractional part of a total product. Earlier man saw himself involved in a total undertaking – making a bow, completing a hunt, growing a crop. The industrial process often makes the individual one in a collection of functions. No one of these functions may give significance to his existence.

There is an increasing load of sheerly intellectual knowledge that is set before man to be mastered as the condition of his existence in a fiercely competitive order of industrial work and political relationships. The accumulation was given an impetus with the invention of printing, and to this facility have now been added many forms of visual aids, electronic dissemination of information, and so on. The atmosphere quivers with messages between all sorts of human groups – intellectual, economic, cultural, political, religious. Satellites, made to orbit in space, now make it possible for a thousand million persons to view in graphic form an event transmitted visually from one hemisphere to another. Preoccupation with this growing mass of information leads to what has been called the "sclerosis of consciousness" – the hardening of mental arteries against forms of personal activity except the severely intellectual.

Along with these developments of personal existence is the uncertainty of survival. Karl Jaspers notes that throughout past history death, in a sense, was voided for the individual. He was assured of survival in his children, or through the permanent community to which he belonged, or through the trees that he planted for posterity. Now, says Jaspers, this continuity is severed for more and more people all over the globe, and the uprooted ones find their native communities growing feebler and themselves becoming detached from the soil where their forebears lie buried.[8]

Can man hope to "sound through" these and other conditions that threaten what it means to be a "person"?

Cassirer does not look on this question merely from the Olympian heights of the scholar abstracted from the world of nature and history. In one of his last writings, *The Myth of the State* (1946), he looked closely at the inevitability of mythic forces in the life of man, whatever the form of a given political structure. Further, in his *The Logic of the Humanities* he noted this: "Civilization is no harmonious self-enclosed whole, but is filled with the most violent inner tensions. . . . For all that it has created it threatens to tear apart again with its own hands." [9] The realization of freedom, which he asserts is the condition of happiness, rests not on technical dominance over nature but man's moral mastery of himself. And as the cultural process develops, the created shows itself to be the enemy of the creator.

The legend of the rabbi Eisik of Cracow teaches that the real treasure is not distant from us but is buried in the intimate parts of our own house – in our own being. As it was the foreign captain who pointed to the location of that treasure, in like manner it may be the experience of the encounter of cultures on the widest scale that points us toward a deepened sense of value and the forms in which these values are symbolized. The formative process is as universal as the human being. The capacity to replace a mere passive receptivity of a chaos of sensuous impressions with symbolic forms is the hallmark of the personal. "Myth and art, language and science," asserts Cassirer, "are in this sense configurations *towards* being: they are not simple copies of an existing reality but represent the main directions of the spiritual movement, of the ideal process by which reality is constituted for us as one and many – as a diversity of forms which are ultimately held together by a unity of meaning." [10]

What can be traced as a process in the history of mankind in personal response to inexhaustible potentials of spirit is to be traced also in the maturation of the child as he moves from self-centered individuality toward responsible personhood. This movement is toward what Pierre Teilhard de Chardin calls the "omega point," as there is seen emerging a race of sentient, responsible, and creative beings.[11]

Chapter III

Communication and Communion

In *Émile,* Jean Jacques Rousseau recounts from Herodotus a story about Darius when he was engaged in a campaign against the Scythians. The king of the Scythians sent to Darius a gift – a bird, a frog, a mouse, and five arrows. The king's ambassador deposited the gift without a word, then withdrew. Forthwith Darius removed his army from that country with all speed, for his captain convinced him that the unspoken meaning of this gift was as follows – unless you become birds and fly up in the sky, or mice and hide in the earth, or frogs and leap into the lake, you will be shot by these arrows and never return home!

Human civilization is dependent upon signs and systems of signs. While animals do respond to signs and signals, such signs do not have the complexity and elaboration of the devices men use. To be sure, the very elaboration of systems of signs creates new problems in a mass society, and the multiplication of signs and their impact on human beings gives added importance to the whole matter of communication and the possible levels of communication.

The cinema has been characterized as giving " truth twenty-four times per second " – referring, of course, to the fact that film is run through the projector at the speed of twenty-four frames per second. The separate images of each frame flow into a continuous and unified impression that possesses unique power for both naturalistic description and for imagination.

The cinema is one of many powerful sources of modern communication, and it is unnecessary to recount the various other forms of printed materials and electronically transmitted images.

One result of the impact of these floods of information and propaganda is the phenomenon of "compressionism." Laurence Kitchin describes the "pervasively weighed-down, boxed-in feeling in modern man," which has been powerfully set forth particularly in dramas for stage and for the cinema screen. It is the theme of Sartre's play *No Exit,* in which three people are forced to exist in the unblinking gaze of each other, and which closes with, "Hell is other people." [1] In the cinema presentation of *Goldfinger,* one conspirator is compressed into the small cube into which his car has been kneaded – compressionism indeed! But little more dramatic, in the intent of this work, than the human situation in general, due to the enforced intimacies of communication without encounter, of multiplied information with little of communion. The technical use of the term "compressionism" is relatively new; the fact is present wherever there is the endeavor to relate love, truth, and power, to aid little men to know human living in a big society.

The new technology has no more critical point in its use than the dangers and the potentialities inherent in the new agencies of communication. The clever, contriving mind of man has led to the use of the term *homo faber,* "the fabricating one." *Homo faber* continues to demonstrate his cleverness with the highly sophisticated devices and inventions that come from his imagination and skills. Prophets of the immediate future have drawn graphic word pictures of the power that Big Brother can come to exert through control of agencies of communication. Who controls the printed page, and radio and film, and to what end, is indeed a crucial question. Charles Morris says this:

> They may be used for the enslavement of the individual or for the enlargement of the sphere of the individual's creative

> participation in society. They may be the means by which beliefs and values and actions of the individual are dictated "from above," or the ways by which the individual is given the material out of which he can form his own opinions, preferences, and conduct.[2]

The signs and symbols by which men live may be manipulated by totalitarian forces for ulterior purposes of a state or society. But there are still other barriers to shared communication that come into existence without planned intent. For example, there is the outcome of the highly specialized knowledge of modern intellectual disciplines. There has been concern with what is known as "the two cultures" — the diverging fields in modern learning of the sciences and the humanities.

Even within a given field such as science there are such high degrees of specialization that communication becomes difficult. Experts within a narrow discipline are able to talk only to each other. Certain educational institutions, aware of the dangers of undereducated experts, provide now for a broader-based knowledge, with a healthy mingling of the humanities and science. But the inherent tendency of specialized disciplines is that each becomes more and more imperious in its demands in the presence of inexhaustible reality. This fact poses problems for cultures trying to achieve a viable degree of unity.

If it is difficult to bridge the gap between the sciences and the humanities, how much more so to communicate across the abyss separating those with a belief in and experience of the sacred, and those for whom existence is essentially profane.

In 1917 a book was published with the title *The Idea of the Holy* (*Das Heilige*). The author of this notable publication, Rudolf Otto, found at the center of authentic religion, of whatever variety, a sense of divine power — the "numinous." It is this experience of the "wholly other" that leads to the unique experience of the Holy, he maintained. Resounding Latin phrases were used by Otto to characterize, insofar as mere words can, the awe flowing from the experience of the numinous — the *mysterium tremendum,* the *mysterium fascinans.* It is in the presence of this power that man feels that he is but dust and ashes. There is, he feels, a sphere transcendent to the physical world. There is a sacred reality, the man with religious experience is convinced, of the invisible entering into the visible.

The religious convictions about the " wholly other " may in our time be displaced by wholly secularistic outlooks. " God is dead " is proclaimed in Nietzsche's *Thus Spake Zarathustra.* What he put bluntly into so many words has been voiced directly and indirectly by many others. The nature of the physical universe as now depicted seems to have no place for a God who is " out there." Recent astronomical theories lead to revised theories of the origins of the visible universe. The fact that the distant galaxies seem to be receding at enormous speeds suggests that the process started with a " big bang " as matter came together to generate cataclysmic energies of this explosion. In time the matter that is now being dissipated through space, impelled by that explosion, will anew come together again, under the inexorable pull of gravity, to start another cycle of this endless process. The time of one cycle, one astronomer calculates, is eighty-two billion years!

These recent theories about our physical universe will be subject to further study and revision. The present conclusions may be challenged as to their basis in physical fact. But one thing seems unquestionable – popular knowledge of our world and the universe of which it is a minute part is such that there is demanded a new level of understanding and a deepened apprehension as to spirit and life.

Symbolic forms may be seen to be indispensable means of communication to the human spirit. If they confirm that there are images of reality to be discerned through symbols, this fact may account for the fierce intensity with which response is made to being grasped by these symbols. For symbols are both of things we know and of things we do not know. It is significant that in the agelong history of the development of symbols, one insistent and constant use is with respect to the fact of death. In no sphere have symbols been more basically used than in religion – man's response to what is his ultimate concern, and his approach to what Otto calls the "wholly other."

Communication has many levels, through signs, signals, symbols, metaphors, and all that belongs to the apprehension of our image worlds. But there is an allied term related to communication – "communion."

Rituals and myths in primitive life are potent channels for a sense of communion. Members of a tribe or clan, in sharing the powerful influence of movement of dance or age-old myths, experience a sense of oneness with their fellows and with their gods; "communion" is not too strong a term to use for this experience. So important is this experience that ritual of an elaborate sort is carried on with the most meticulous care; no risk must be taken that would prejudice its potent influence. The rites, whether celebrating the seasons, or victory, or another point of importance to existence for the people, give the strong sense of solidarity with each other and of unity with unseen and partially understood transhuman powers. Rites have been called the motor manifestations of psychic life. They give dynamic form to feelings and emotions that reach to the deepest levels of the self.

Nor is such dramatic and dynamic expression restricted to the life of primitive man. Ritual and myth are equally indispensable in developed societies and cultures. Whitehead points out that symbolism remains in government even when its functions have been reduced to the utmost simplicity. And in the event of undue simplification, he adds, "private clubs and associations at once commence to reconstitute symbolic actions." And this is not mere masquerade, for the object of symbolism is the enhancement of the importance of what is symbolized.[3]

The symbolisms of rites and myths are indispensable resources for communication in depth – a depth aptly expressed by the term "communion." Nor is this level only for archaic or primitive men. One has only to think of the potency for communism of the myth of a classless society or for the Christian of the myth of Creation – both powerful convictions that go beyond what can neatly be formulated in discursive terms.

There is a further area of a form of communication that can be deserving of the term "communion" – *art*. The experience of those who have stood before the paintings in the caves of Dordogne and Lascaux in Europe is not only of admiration and awe at these achievements. Across the long centuries and millennia since those unknown and vanished men created these forms in the silent depths of ageless caves, there is a feeling of common humanity. The purpose of these archaic men cannot be fully known, but there is a timelessness about the genius of their graphic expression that puts the viewer into communion with the spirit and the skill of hand which accounted for these creations.

One might ask this question: What accounts for the fact that a Rembrandt painting could be valued (in commercial terms) at over two million dollars? The materials of canvas, frame, and pigments are purchasable at a trifling sum. Yet this painting is priceless. So with a masterpiece such as the *Mona Lisa* and many others. It is not a matter of so many dollars. If such works should be destroyed the loss that would be felt would go far too deep for any financial accounting. So it was when a vandal cut off the head of the bronze statue of the maiden that gazes out over the harbor of Copenhagen. The tears that people shed over this act attested a feeling of irreparable loss. Some transcendent element is present in the material components of these works of art. Only so can the depth of these feelings be accounted for.

One writer calls the work of art "the intercessional factor in this our sensuous world, unifying and transcending the competing and frustrating trends of human desire." And from the standpoint of literature as art, Allen Tate says that literature does not communicate and cannot; rather, the work of literature is a participation in communion. He continues: "Perhaps it is not too grandiose a conception to suggest that works of literature, from the short lyric to the long epic, are the recurrent discovery of the human communion *as experience*, in a definite place and at a definite time." [4]

Not only in art is there the level of communion as a deep level of communication. A significant statement was made by a Russian scientist: "I do not imagine God as he is depicted on icons. To me God is a sort of spiritual principle, the stimulus of the emergence of the galaxies, the stars, the planets, and of everything which lives and reproduces on these planets, from the most elementary cells up to men." [5] The outlook set forth here is a possible step toward seeing the universe as much more than an infinite mechanism; indeed, there is reflected in the statement an incipient sense of communion between this spiritual principle and the spirit of man.

The term "passionate" is not often associated with natural science. Yet for one natural scientist it is a basic term. Michael Polanyi in his *Personal Knowledge* asserts that it is the passionate note which makes science function like other constituents of culture, such as art, religion, morality, and law. He adds:

> Scientific passion serves [also] as a guide in the assessment of what is of higher and what of lesser interest; what is great in science and what relatively slight. I want to show that this appreciation depends ultimately on a sense of intellectual beauty; that it is an emotional response which can never be dispassionately defined, any more than we can dispassionately define the beauty of a work of art or the excellence of a noble action.[6]

In this twentieth century, are there authentic symbols that provide for genuine communication between men and with ultimate reality? It seems clear that many of the old symbols are dead. But symbolic power will exist as long as the spirit of man searches for genuine values, for authentic selfhood, for images of reality. Despite all that has been created by way of technological mastery of physical force, it becomes clear that all is not going well. There have been two world wars in this century. There is a profound sense of alienation and loss of identity and homelessness on the part of growing numbers whose existence is cast in the impersonal mass of urban cities, and whose living comes through mechanically carrying out tasks with limited meaning.

There is no substitute for the power of symbols, man's nature being what it is. For the symbol, it is claimed, is the clue to the human and the organon of humanity. Yet to be authentic, symbols must be *living*.

In the Church of the Ascension in New York City, there is a handsome mural showing a literal depiction of that event as described in the New Testament. The central figure, Christ, has left the earth and is moving toward the upper realms, with the disciples, earthbound, gazing at their departing Savior.

This imagery is entirely natural to the three-story world of Biblical times. How shall this doctrine with its profound meaning be made to have its authentic symbolic power to men and women and youth of this space age? Paul Tillich states the case: "The great art of the religious educator is to transform the primitive literalism of the religious symbols into a conceptual interpretation without destroying the power of the symbols." [7]

Symbols have had no more telling expression than in religion. And in no phase of his experience has there been greater possibility of man's being overwhelmed by his symbolic accessories. There has been a recurring mood of iconoclasm in various periods of the history of the church, and the recurring fact of sweeping out of signs and symbols in order to clarify the image of religious reality. Yet even the utter simplicity of a Quaker service of worship has its own symbolism. The outreach of finite beings toward Being is given multiform expression in the response to the *mysterium tremendum.* Certain primitive tribes interpret the appearance of a rainbow as the attempt of their gods to reach down to them in communication. Their response is to shoot arrows toward the shimmering light as their own attempt to establish some channel of openness with the transcendent forces that they believe to be manifested in the rainbow.[8] In the account given in Genesis the bow in the heavens was a sign of the " everlasting covenant between God and every living creature " (Gen. 9:16).

What may be more likely to attract the attention and thought of modern man than a bow in the sky is the contrail of a soaring rocket. In the achievement of the conquest of space he finds the fascination that in another age might have been called forth by the wonders of nature and the liturgies of worship. The power of the dynamo and the unearthly glow of the nuclear reactor are facts that seem to put fancy to flight. Symbols of a living faith may be wrought from the conviction that techniques of the creative hand and mind of man are his chief dependence.

There is the further problem of making vivid to the mind of modern man the imagery that was natural in the views held of the world in earlier ages. One instance has already been cited — the response that might be made to a painting of the Ascension of Christ. Some scholars urge the impossibility of making these old images a living reality, that the only way to a symbolism with living religious meaning is by means of demythologization — frankly discarding as outmoded the patterns of thought that were the natural ones to a premodern age. Ideas of this nature account in part for the phenomenal interest in a book such as *Honest to God* by Bishop Robinson.

If there is to be religious communication to modern man, it will not be by means of attempting to impose a framework of thought no longer possible for him. Nor will it come by dressing up liturgies with more elaborate forms. For authentic religious symbols must come from man's encounter with the ultimate. They must be generated from the living awareness that God is not a symbol but the ground of all Being. Symbols are born of living encounter; they die when that living experience is no more, and what is left is a fossil. This is more than reason can compass.

Yet this may be of little help for those unable to grasp the meaning of anything transcendent to what can be heard, felt, and seen. There is needed another dimension of understanding.

One may be found in art. It has been called "the layman's mystery" (*le mystère laïc*). Many persons to whom the religious is apparently shut off will respond in an almost religious way to the authentic power of meaningful art. And as indicated above, in authentic art there is a concrete manifestation of the transcendent, integrally a part of the material components – a vision through the stone of the sculptor that has yielded to his hand and imagination the hidden power of a statue such as Rodin's *Man of Primal Times,* or the superlative power of paintings such as those of Rouault.

Another source of help to modern man seemingly insulated from the religious symbol is through the experience of an *I* in encounter with a *thou.* Martin Buber put many in his debt in his discussion of the difference between an I-thou relation and an I-it relation. The word *I,* he pointed out in his book *I and Thou,* cannot be used alone. But a great difference is made whether it is combined with an *it* or with a *thou.*

A translation of Job 6:14 by Moffatt reads thus: "Friends should be kind to a despairing man, or he will give up faith in the Almighty." This implies that there is a social basis for encounter with the infinite thou. In somewhat more philosophical terms, Karl Jaspers says:

> One of man's supreme achievements is the genuine communication from person to person, when from out of their historical situation in their search for the ultimate meaning of existence, the Transcendent breaks into thought, revealing to each the authenticity of his Selfhood and their common ground in the Encompassing.[9]

The conditions of authentic communication between man and the Divine, between finite beings and the Eternal, were set forth by the prophets of the Old Testament and given final expression, in the view of the Christian faith, in the New Testament.

Isaiah poured fine scorn on those who would worship that which came from the hands of the smith and the carpenter: "Shall I fall down to the stock of a tree?" (Isa. 44:10 ff.). As Cassirer says, "The Prophetic world is visible only in the religious idea and can be encompassed in no mere image which is oriented solely toward the sensuous present and remains confined within it." [10] In the New Testament is the summary conviction that in Christ men found "the image of the invisible God" (Col. 1:15). And in the two thousand years of subsequent history of this religious tradition, there is the most informative effort to relate the invisible reality of God to the visible realities of men. Communication, communion, religious symbols – all find expression here.

Chapter IV

Forms of Culture

When a sculptor looks at a block of marble, he sees more than stone. Within that formless body of inert material he envisages living shape. By the power of his vision and the skill of his hand liberation is given to that sleeping form. Through the transforming insight of the artist, there comes into being a reality that otherwise would have remained everlastingly dormant.

In Auguste Rodin's *Man of Primal Times* there are bodied forth the gestures and movements of awakening. The powerful figure shown in the shape that came from the sculptor is rousing to begin the work of unnumbered centuries — "work that has no measure and no end," to use a characterization of this masterpiece by Rainer Maria Rilke. The hand of the figure, still heavy with the long slumber of the ages, rests on top of the head. The figure is that of a man of primal times, but he is beginning to be aware of the stirring of feeling that makes him more than physical being.

The sculptor makes the inanimate marble come alive with expression. This liberation of what slumbered there until his chisel, hand, and insight joined to create a masterpiece of powerful beauty is akin to the liberation of spirit that is open to humanity through symbolic forms.

Symbolic expression may come through sensuous material. The sculptor uses marble. The painter is dependent on pigments, canvas, brush, and palette knife. Music, the most metaphysical of the arts, still depends on instruments of some kind.

Or the symbolizing may rest on inner activity – the mythic response to existence expressed through age-old tales and rites, the endless forms of human language that yet have a common linguistic function that is universal, the expression of religious faith and aspiration through symbol as a channel from the finite to the infinite, and the invisible forces dealt with by science through sign and symbol. These are some of the symbolic forms that have marked the ways of man's progressive self-liberation.

Each symbolic form has its own characteristics. Yet they have in their totality a shared import and meaning. In them is seen, in Goethe's words, a synthesis of world and spirit. We look now at the symbolic forms given particular emphasis by Cassirer.

Mythical Consciousness and the Mythic Search

Persistence of Mythmaking. In the Greek drama *Choephoroi,* by Aeschylus, there is a prayer by Electra at the grave of Agamemnon; the prayer calls on the dread spirits who dwell below the earth, and also on

> Earth our Mother, who doth all things breed,
> and nurse, and takes again to her their seed.

Embodied in these lines is the implicit belief that Earth is the common mother who brings the sons of men to light; they are given back to her at death, to be resurrected to new life in the cycle of becoming.

This is part of a very widespread mythical view that interprets the relation of Heaven and Earth as that of Father and Mother. This is made clear in the mythologies of many peoples. The Greek myths of creation told of a race of Titans that resulted from the union of *Uranos* and *Gaia,* or Heaven and Earth. In what is now New Zealand the Polynesians had a similar myth of creation. The names differed: Heaven and Earth were called *Ranga* and *Papa.* But the myths of these widely separated places and peoples had a close resemblance.

There is a Vedic hymn of creation showing how the social orders were accounted for by being made of different parts of *Purusha:* his mouth became the Brahmin; his arms, the warrior; his thighs, the trader and the farmer; and his feet, the servile class.

So archaic men throughout the world had their mythical accounts of the origins of all things. The mass of literature setting forth the mythologies of different peoples and tribes is enormous. The record makes plain the fact that the mythical consciousness has been essentially universal, and the mythic search a most persistent one.

But the definition of "myth" is not simple. From one viewpoint it is taken to mean that which is merely legendary or fanciful with no foundation in fact or reason. But from another viewpoint it is the very mainspring of culture.

It is easily supposed in our age of the dominance of science that myth can be disregarded as merely the by-product of infantile cultures. Auguste Comte (1798–1857) described three stages of man's cultural development: he rose from primitive consciousness, to theoretical knowledge, then to a spiritual domination of reality. The three stages, as Comte described them, were the theological, the metaphysical, and the positive. In the first stage, man's subjective desires were turned into demons and gods. In the second stage, he transformed them into abstract concepts. And in the third stage, man confronts empirical reality. Once a higher stage is reached, the preceding one is no longer needed.

A look at another Greek myth, however, points to persistent meanings and significance. The account of Acteon, the hunter, parallels in a thought-provoking way a meaning of the modern unveiling of secrets of atomic power.

According to the ancient story, Acteon on Mt. Kitharon saw Artemis, goddess of chastity, bathing. In outrage at the invasion of her privacy, she changed him into a stag; in this form, he was chased by his own hounds, run down, and killed. A present-day writer asks whether a kindred fate awaits men who have dared unveil the naked facts of nuclear power. He poses the as yet unanswered question asked in George Bernard Shaw's *Don Juan:* " And is man any the less destroying himself, for all this boasted brain of his? " [1]

A response to this persistent question might be made in the words of still another Greek myth – that of Prometheus. He dared the wrath of Zeus to bring the gift of fire to men. For his temerity he was punished by being chained to a rock; eagles fed on his liver by day, consuming what grew back in the night. The timeless courage of Prometheus is shown in Aeschylus' drama, in which Prometheus says:

> There is no torture and no cunning trick,
> There is no force which can compel my speech,
> Unless Zeus wills to loose these deadly bonds.
> So let him hurl his deadly thunderbolt,
> And with the white wings of the snow,
> With lightning and with earthquake,
> Confound the reeling world.
> None of this will bend my will.

To this the Herald says, " Submit, you fool, submit. In agony learn wisdom." The reply gives a timeless measure of the durability of will:

> Seek to persuade the sea wave not to break.
> You will persuade me no more easily.[2]

The living potency of myth in modern times is illustrated by its use in the rise of Hitler's Nazi movement in Germany. Cassirer, who himself became a refugee from Nazism, says that " The real rearmament (of Germany) began with the rise of the political myths. The later military rearmament was only an accessory after the fact." [3]

It is well known that Hitler was fascinated by Wagnerian operas and their musical depiction of the epic myths of the Nibelungenlied. To him, music and myth seemed to foreshadow a glory that was to last a thousand years! Here was mythic thinking in the worst sense – the power of whose wild assertions proved too much for the conscious mind of multitudes who were swept into the Nazi movement. But the potency of political myth is not restricted to totalitarian powers. Cassirer says that politics dwells on volcanic soil, and makes this observation:

> In all critical moments of man's social life, the rational forces that resist the rise of the old mythical conceptions are no longer sure of themselves. In these moments, the time for myth has come again. For myth has not been really vanquished and subjugated. It is always there, lurking in the dark, and waiting for its hour and opportunity. This hour comes as the other binding forces of man's social life, for one reason or another, lose their strength and are no longer able to combat the demonic mythical powers.[4]

Myth, then, has permanent as well as primitive aspects. Along with man's accumulating load of conscious knowledge, he still experiences the *mysterium tremendum.* In certain moments, the ritual and mythology, which once dominated conscious life, may well up in almost uncontrolled power from subterranean levels of the unconscious. The power of the Nazi myth came in part from the depiction of an apocalyptic battle, in which all must perish and from which another world would be born. In Marxism there is indubitable potency in the absolute goal of history, the Golden Age of a classless society, a redemption to be reached through changes effected by the sufferings of the proletariat. In present-day China, the life of the communes is galvanized by appeals to the example of Wu Sung, a hero of the famed Chinese classic, *Shui Hu Chuan,* and each worker is urged to do battle " single spear, single horse " like that hero of old. And no one acquainted with political realities in so-called democracies can be in doubt of the part played by mythologies of political parties in affecting voting decisions.

Permanent myth persists. Reinhold Niebuhr has observed

that "neither the vital thrust of life, nor its organic unities nor its disharmonies nor its highest possibilities can be expressed in terms of logical and rational consistency." [5] There are outgrown superstitions that deserve to be called "only a myth." But the mythic search will not cease for finite beings, and not all mysteries can be transformed into problems.

Sources of Myth. To speak of sources of this symbolic form is to bring into imaginative view a vast background. In Cassirer's *The Philosophy of Symbolic Forms* the entire second volume is on the mythical consciousness. The liberation of logical functions and personal awareness came from the matrix of prehistoric myth. Thomas Mann has said that the ego detaches itself from the mythical collective in the same way that certain figures of Rodin wrest themselves from the stone and awaken from it.

The fantasies of imaginative primitive minds have had a rich array of raw materials in natural symbols — sun and moon, day and night, seasons and tides, the surging flow of animal life. A modern painting such as Burchfield's *The Night Wind* is a reminder of how close to sophisticated man are the responses to raw forces of nature. The poetic powers of the early storyteller wove fascinating tales from myths with cosmic meanings.

In the original relations between man and animals there was a strong element of magic. Large animals, such as the elephant, tiger, and rhinoceros, were supposed to have supernatural powers. Hunting was interweaving of techniques of the chase with magical attitudes toward the quarry. The use of animal forms in rock carvings and in cave paintings give evidence of how strong were totemistic feelings between man and animal, and how much of hidden clues to existence he found in them.

In medieval Europe an elaborate set of symbols developed around animals, real or fabulous. A chief source of bestiaries was an ancient work, *Physiologus.* In the Orient there was also an elaborate symbolism based on animal forms. In Chinese thought the dragon visually demonstrated the essence of ritualistic principles; it stood for the East and for Spring, as the tiger stood for the West and for Autumn. The phoenix was the essence of the *yang* principle, and the *chi-lin* was a herald of peace and prosperity. "In the early stages of the world-view," says Cassirer, "there is as yet no sharp boundary separating man from the totality of living things, from the world of animals and plants; particularly in totemism the kinship between man and animal, and above all the relation between a clan and its totem animal or plant, is taken by no means in a figurative but in a strictly literal sense." [6]

For another thing, the mythical consciousness was a way of bringing some structure and order to beliefs. In this the place of ritual was basic. Ritual has been called a sanctified habit system. For primitive man it was a precious means of assurance of not sliding into the waiting abyss of the unknown. It was a satisfaction to do all humanly possible to propitiate forces beyond rational understanding, with the solidarity of the total community represented in meticulously wrought rites.

But the power of ritual as an expression of the mythical consciousness is not as mere representation. It is not a mere imitative portrayal of an event, for the image *is* identical with the thing. As Cassirer says, "Seen in this light, rites are not originally 'allegorical'; they do not merely copy or represent but are absolutely *real;* they are so woven into the reality of action as to form an indispensable part of it." [7]

On occasion there may be the development of a cult that is a response to despair. Thus the peyote cult of the American Southwest is interpreted as a despairing response to being deprived of long-accepted modes of tribal living because of the encroachment of the white man. A recent manifestation of this response is the bursting into existence of the Nazi myths, in part an outgrowth of acceptance of the pessimism of Spengler's views on the decline of the West. While imposed from above, the rites had the hypnotic power of ordered movement; and the chants, salutes, and all the paraphernalia of the ritual added to the organic movements of a tribe the technological enlargement of modern equipment.

Another instance of mythical consciousness in present-day living is seen in the "cargo cults" of certain regions of Oceania. There, primitive peoples have seen an unparalleled wealth of material things, including food, brought to their shores in unimaginable profusion because of war or commerce. The belief of the cargo cults is that their own ships will soon appear on the horizon; the assurance of survival and the escape from hard work will thus come through miraculous agencies.

There has been, then, a mutual dependence between myth and ritual, with the mythical becoming the "theology" of the acts. In early Europe religious dancers on the altar of the White Goddess assured by their turnings (whence our *verses* of poetry for the *versus* of their movements) their living commentary-in-movement on the grand theme of the life, death, and resurrection of the Spirit of the Year. Professor Clyde Kluckhohn makes this comment: "Myth is a constant by-product of a living faith which is in need of miracles; of sociological status which demands precedents, or moral rule which requires sanction."[8]

Characteristics of Living Myth. Language and myth developed together. But the assertion of reason through the further development of language brought to the mythical consciousness a searching critique. Cassirer has delineated the interrelationships of language and myth. Many of the primitive mythologies disappear. But the mythical consciousness persists, and the mythic search must persist for finite beings in the presence of World, absolute and infinite.

Myth has been one of the forms in which men have sought to know their world. These things can be said of persistent myth:

Myth is addressed to the whole man, and the mythic understanding seeks a coherent structure out of the encounter of himself and his people with his world. The whole man confronts a living "thou" in nature; and the whole man – emotional and imaginative as well as intellectual – gives expression to the experience.

The myth, to be truly mythical in its power, must be believed in. It is not a matter of mere fantasy. "Real myth," Martin Buber observed, "is the expression not of an imaginative state of mind or of mere feeling but of a real meeting of two Realities."

The myth is cosmically significant. It is an attempt to enlarge the immediacies of existence. The essential imagery of a people's myths reflects their attempt to embrace the realities that transcend the powers of discursive reason. To ask about the creation of the world is to explore a reality that the mind cannot comprehend but that is inescapable as a question for finite persons. To inquire about "last things" in a world that is in the process of constant change is to have recourse in mythic apprehension of realities that cannot be forged into a conceptual whole. It is obvious that myth, however primitive its origins, has an indispensable place as one of the symbolic forms of man's existence.

It is ironical that the one term "myth" has to do service for almost diametrically opposite meanings: that which has no foundation as when we speak of "a mere myth," and that which points to ultimate meanings. Few subjects have, within recent theological and philosophical thought, had more intensive and sustained consideration than the religious dimensions of the mythic search.

Two things may be said at this point about the mythical consciousness and the mythic search. The whole vast field of myth is not a form of misunderstanding. Rather it has, as Susanne Langer puts it, a positive significance in its origins of archaic forms of understanding. "In its origins"—for as has been pointed out, the religious dimensions of myth in the experience of the most sophisticated of men make the mythic search a continuing and irreplacable necessity.

The second observation is that the mythic search, at whatever stage, is not a mere reflection of reality. It is not a kind of mirror that is represented by consciousness or spirit. "The act of consciousness which gives birth to one or another of these forms, to science, to art, to language (and myth), does not simply discover and reproduce an ensemble of pre-existent objects" asserts Ashley Montagu. Rather, all forms brought into being by the mind are due to a spontaneous act, a creative force, in the Kantian sense.[9]

Cassirer shows the range of the mythic search in these words: "The very lowest, most primitive mythical configuration proves to be a vehicle of meaning for it already stands in the sign of that primordial division which raises the world of the sacred from the world of the profane. . . . But on the other hand even the highest religious truth remains attached to sensuous existence, to the world of images as well as things."[10]

Language as Symbolic Form

Power of the Name. Language has been characterized as the most momentous and the most mysterious product of the human mind. *Thought* and *Word* are brought together in the familiar words that open the Gospel of John, "In the beginning was the Word." The original term, *logos,* means both word, in the literal sense, and the power of order in the world, with still deeper meanings for Christian theology.

Language and myth developed together in man's experience through untold ages. Early forms of language were presumably those of pure expression. Animals have a kind of vocabulary of expressive sounds for communication with their kind; some of these, as with dolphins, seem remarkably elaborate. Yet there is a profound difference between their reactions to signs and signals and the human response to symbols. As the myth confronted early man with a preformed world of symbolic interpretation, so did language, through *name* and *story* and all other linguistic experience become basic in the unfolding of his understanding.

Writing of Bushmen in Africa, Laurens Van der Post asserts that for these people their stories are their dearest possession. The Bushman will generously share his most precious material treasure – water. But he is instantly on guard if approached to share a story from his people. Mr. Van der Post says: "It was only after many days, when he had come to trust us more, that he confessed to having stories, and told us some of them; but even so I always felt that there was deep in his heart a story of stories, which needed far more time and sharing of experience than I could afford just then." [11]

The *name* and its power shows a strong link between myth and language. The folktale of Rumpelstiltskin reflects belief that knowing a name may prove to be a key to power over another person. The power of a name is suggested in this passage from Euripides' *Iphigenia in Tauris*. Iphigenia asks Orestes, "Are ye two of one mother born?" This leads to the following exchange:

> Orestes: No, not in blood. In love we are brothers sworn.
> Iphigenia: Thou also hast a name. Tell me thereof.
> O: Call me Unfortunate. 'Tis name enough.
> I: I asked not that. Let that with Fortune lie.
> O: Fools cannot laugh at them that nameless die.
> I: Why grudge me this? Hast thou such mighty fame?
> O: My body, if thou wilt, but not my name.[12]

A child just beginning to learn the mother tongue (a significant term in itself) has a thirst to know the names of things – a desire that can become almost obsessive. There is a classic passage from the life of Helen Keller that tells of the occasion when this blind and deaf child discovered immeasurable release through being enlightened that each thing had a name. As she and her teacher walked past the well house, someone there was drawing water. The teacher placed the child's hand so that the cool water would flow over it. Miss Keller says in her autobiography:

> As the cold stream gushed over my hand she spelled into the other w-a-t-e-r, first slowly then rapidly. I stood still, my whole attention fixed upon the motion of her fingers. Suddenly, I felt a misty consciousness as of something forgotten – a

> thrill of returning thought; and somehow the mystery of language was revealed to me. I knew then that w-a-t-e-r meant the wonderful something that was flowing over my hand. That living word awakened my soul, gave it light, joy, hope, set it free. There were barriers still, it is true, but barriers that in time could be swept away.

The story of this incident is carried a step farther in these words:

> I left the well-house, eager to learn. Everything had a name, and each name gave birth to a new thought. As we returned to the house every object which I touched seemed to quiver with life. This was because I saw everything with the strange new sight that had come to me.[13]

In the Biblical account of the wrestling of Jacob with the angel, Jacob says to his adversary, " Tell me, I pray thee, thy name." This reflects the mythic conviction that possession of the name was the key to control, since it was the essence of the reality of the adversary himself. There is also an early Biblical account of the meaning of man's relation to the animals, in that he gave them their names: " So out of the ground the Lord God formed every beast of the field and every bird of the air, and brought them to the man to see what he would call them; and whatever the man called every living creature, that was its name " (Gen. 2:19). To be able to name a name (whether of animal or any object) is to fix that object in experience permanently. The name has symbolic power.

Language and Symbol. Language as a symbolic form manifests the fact that man has his own indispensable part to play in the achievement of reason. It is not a primitive ready-made endowment. Each language has a history. Its origins are lost in prehistory. Some have maintained that there is a direct path from the emotional expressions of interjection, akin to animals' signals, to speech. But other students of the subject point out the profound differences between animal utterance and human speech. Language manifests a dimension different in kind from emotional expression.

Words are symbols. They are not mere copies of something else. In linguistic form there is manifested another instance of an activity that is not a mere replica of something already existing.

The experience of the child in mastering his mother tongue recapitulates what must have been in some measure the relation of archaic man to language. The ability to relate name and object, and to express meaning in even elementary phrases, has its indispensable place in refining the perception and observation of the child. His unfettered fancies take on order. The unrestricted leaps of the imagination are tamed and controlled.

The power of personification so well manifested in the teller of mythical tales or in the poet, for whom any object tended to take a personal shape, came to be subject in some degree to logic. The purely subjective function of expression of feeling became elaborated into the process of language.

The connection between " word " and " thing " still remains somewhat mysterious. Especially is this true for those whose language has the strikingly suggestive form of ideographs, as with Chinese and Japanese. The archaic forms of these characters were literally pictographs, much as were the hieroglyphics of ancient written languages of the Middle East. The relation of hieroglyph and object was a literal correspondence, though even with these symbolism soon developed. The original Chinese character for " moon " was a literal representation of its crescent shape. That form is still faintly retained in the curving line of the character. And there are differences between various languages in the mode of expressing a given object. Thus the Greek word for " moon," *men,* literally means " the measurer," while the Latin *luna* has its root in the meaning of " light." In ideographic languages much stress is laid on calligraphy, through which the verve of vital form is added, by the artistic impulse, to the intelligible meaning – a unique symbolic relation of the sensuous and the intelligible.

In numerous instances there can be seen the early connection between the mythical consciousness and language. The active power of words is reflected in curses, oracles, and incantations. In Ovid's *Metamorphoses* occurs this line: "By magic songs and incantations even the moon can be dragged down from heaven." The mythic power of language easily leads to the corruption of hardly won exactness of meaning. The instance of "Nazi Deutsch" is cited by Cassirer in his *Myth of the State*. It was characterized by the twisting of meanings of familiar terms and the coining of new terms to carry the ideology of the Nazi regime. An accompanying ritual was developed, and the author adds that "since in the totalitarian state there is no private sphere, independent of political life, the whole life of man is suddenly inundated by a high tide of new rituals." [14]

But language has a way of breaking out of the iron circle of the mythical consciousness. It is through language that persons are able to cross the chasm from specific perceptions to general concepts. It is through the power of the *logos*, the power of logic, that the individual is able to escape from the immediacy of the *here* to the *not here*. Through this symbolic form it is possible to pass from a merely instinctive impulsive cry to ordered speech. *Names* furnish a multiplicity of expression; *sentences* supply powerful vehicles of meaning.

The tracing of the development of language has led some thinkers on linguistics to suppose that the ultimate ideal for language is pure logic, in which each term would have precise meaning and each expression would have the exactness of a mathematical formula. The derived and artificial "language" of scientific formulae is taken to be the model for the natural languages of man.

But the meaning of language is not fully expressed in the power of logic. Poetry has been called the mother tongue of humanity. Poetic metaphor — or any other form of metaphor — means a sharpening of man's associative ability. Martin Foss says: "The spirit of a language is in the process, not in the word, and just because of that the words must enter into a tension which overcomes a fixation and provides a meaning beyond their symbolic and only apparent sufficiency." [15] "Words *express* intuitive meanings, but *state*, or are mere signs of, logical meanings" is the way this is put by Folke Leander.[16] Poetry and metaphor express neither the mythic world of gods and demons nor the logical truth of abstract relations, says Cassirer, but through illusion and fantasy give utterance to the realm of pure feeling.

Art: Its Transforming Images

As a system of communication, art is perhaps even prior to language. The impulse to fill empty space on pots and utensils with decorative design and ornamental figures remains a mute testimony, but an eloquent one, in man's earliest records. There is a special term for what was back of this impulse: *horror vacui*, the dislike of leaving unused the possibilities of empty space.

The tracing of the development of the impulse to express meaningful form in art, as made known in the enormous amount of information on the varied forms of art among the peoples of the world through the ages of prehistory and of history, reveals a kinship of this symbolic form to those of myth and of language. There is a constant interplay between the constructive powers of the person and of surrounding realities — realities transformed by the human response. The mythical consciousness, with its impression of the immediacies of space, time, powers of nature, and all that made up the experience of archaic man, led toward the continuing mythic search that engages modern man. And the development of language, in which *name* and *thing* at first seemed identical in reality and power, led to the ideal significatory function of this symbolic form, under the force of the *logos*, the everlasting Word. A kindred development becomes manifest in the images of the varied art forms. Cassirer says this:

> . . . Art leads us to still another stage of detachment. Here again there is at first no sharp differentiation between the

> ideal and the real; here again the configuration is not initially regarded as the outcome of a creative process, as a pure product of the productive imagination. The beginnings of creative art seem rather to partake of a sphere in which creative activity is still embedded in magical representations and directed toward specific magical *aims,* in which consequently the image itself still has no independent, purely aesthetic significance. And yet in the development of spiritual expression the very first stirrings of artistic activity provide an entirely new beginning, achieve a new principle. Here for the first time the image world acquires a purely *immanent* validity and truth. It does not aim at something else or refer to something else; it simply " is " and consists in itself.[17]

This is a penetrating statement by this thinker, but its meaning might be clearer from some actual images, insofar as words can convey them. Look at a few concrete aspects of developing art forms.

Early Art Forms. One of the most dramatic and powerful examples of early art is the set of paintings discovered in caves in France and in northern Spain, notably at Lascaux and at Altamira. The paintings at Lascaux were stumbled onto by four boys on September 12, 1940. It is estimated that these paintings and engravings were done at least twenty thousand years ago. There is unsurpassable mastery of expression that was given by these Paleolithic men to the forms of bison, panther, horse, aurochs, and other animals. Across the silent millennia they communicate to the modern viewer, even through printed replicas, the human sensitivities of these men of long ago, giving expression to their inner impulses as they created this magnificent art. One of the students of their achievements says that from their art work there emanates a breath of wild and graceful life, giving us today a living sense of the presence of those so far distant in time. He continues:

> There stood before us something nearly of flesh and blood, . . . and also something paradoxical that is characteristic of all prehistoric art. It is not men that we see in the traces that

> distant mankind left us as a mirror of itself. With exceedingly few exceptions, the representations are all of animals. These Lascaux men forcefully transmitted to us the fact that, being men, they resembled us, but as a means for telling us so, they left us innumerable pictures of the animality they were shedding – as though they felt obliged to clothe a nascent marvel with the animal grace they had lost. These non-human figures, wrought with youthful strength, declare not only that they who painted them became full-grown men by painting them, but that they chose animality rather than themselves to give the image that suggests what is fascinating in mankind.[18]

It is unlikely that these amazing works were done just for art's sake. It seems probable that the impulse for their creation came in large measure from magical purposes, since the hunting of the animals shown was important for the physical survival of these early men. Further, there may have been an impulse from the mysterious life of animals, with their grace and beauty and their closeness to nature, that moved early man to preserve these forms in paintings and carvings. The powerful impression made by these works is expressed in these words of characterization by the author quoted above: "That which we hold worthy of our love is always that which overwhelms us; it is the unhoped for, the thing beyond hoping for" (p. 15).

Evidence of this impulse of early man toward creative form has been left in many places. Reproductions akin to those of Lascaux and Altamira are found from northern Norway to southern Africa. In Peruvian caves, also, drawings have been found of animals and their hunters, executed at least ninety-five hundred years ago in dark red, ochre, and green. They were found in 1962 in the Toquepala copper mines.[19]

Among the fifty thousand aborigines still living in Australia, there are well-developed art forms that are entirely indigenous to their life. The motifs of this distinctive art come from their ways of looking and living. In the hard land of the interior of Australia, existence for these aborigines depends on reading expertly the signs on the hard desert floor. Their forms of drawing and painting traditionally have retained the point of view of looking down from above. Within this framework, distinctive designs were created, distinguished by rhythm, balance, and skillful combinations of colors and forms maintained over long millennia.

Further illustrations of this persistent impulse to create art forms are found in the sand paintings of the Navajo Indians. There is a repertory of over a thousand designs in this distinctive medium. The designs reflect a sure awareness of basic principles of design and of color harmonies and of contrasts. The designs body forth, on symbolic altars, personifications of the Wind People, Cloud People, Red Ant People, and others. They were made chiefly for magical, not aesthetic, purposes. But the designs testify to the irrepressible impulse to give symbolic form through significant design.

The joy of creation and the satisfaction of giving significant form to even the most common object is reflected in the gift of a food-stirring paddle, an account preserved by the anthropologist Melville J. Herkovits. He reports that as he was taking leave of a tribe, a woman brought to him this kitchen object, fashioned with consummate loveliness of line and design. As she handed it to him she said: " Take this. Ayobo made this for me before I came to live with him. Put it in the big house in your white man's country where you told me beautiful things are kept. And write on a piece of paper that Ayobo made it." [20] The incident is set forth by the author under the heading " Art and Value." It is clear that for the man and wife whose it was, there was a meaning in this food paddle that went far beyond its utilitarian function and beyond what words could express. It embodied a way of seeing, and incarnated a passion to give outward form to inner vision. This feeling is expressed from another setting as an author describes how, as a lad, he watched an Indian woman in the Southwest absorbed in forming clay bowls, giving plastic expression to her inward vision. This boy saw that " in love, in the new creation of God, there are no copies." He adds: " And I saw and knew that she was beautiful and alive with the joy and freedom of obedient shaping with God, and the bowl was signed forever with grace." [21]

A contemporary expression of the primal impulse to art form is seen in the successive generations of children who, when given freedom, spontaneously paint, draw, and mold with sometimes astonishing creative results. One pioneer in child art, Franz Cizek, has a simple characterization of his method with children: "I take the lid off!" The beginning stages of child drawing and painting can be called scribblings, but, as one observer said, these scribblings are to drawing what bablings are to speech. The child's way of approaching graphic expression make plain that the limits of language are not the boundaries of experience.

Art as Symbolic Form. In the foregoing, chief attention has been given to early forms of art. This was for the reason that here we see in emergent form the separation, and the flowing together, of the sensuous and the intelligible. The painters of the forms in the Lascaux Cave show the most intimate familiarity with the subjects — the animals they depicted. Yet even though their central purpose may have been magic, their aesthetic sense captured the essence, the living form beneath forms, of the running horses and the charging bison.

Art as symbolic form, then, is not mere imitation. Technical mastery may be admirable in getting a likeness, but this is no substitute for the intuition of the form of things. Great art is marked by evidence of an inner spontaneity on the part of the artist as he puts the stamp of his own peculiar vision on the subject. He himself may be unaware of the unconscious sources of that vision, whether the subject is a statue, a painting, a literary creation, or other. In no other symbolic form is the constructive activity of the self more in evidence than in art.

There is clearly an illumination of this fact when one compares the photograph of a landscape, for example, with its rendition by a competent artist. Contrast a photograph of Mont-Sainte-Victoire with the interpretation of this landscape by Cézanne and there is a revelation of his mind in what he has selected, what he has omitted. Set any four artists to work to paint a given landscape. What will result will be four interpretations as each has sought to give form to his particular response to the scene. Art, then, is not imitation of nature, but rather, it is, as Cassirer observes, the discovery of nature.

On this, three further things may be said. The first is that art depends on some measure of abstraction for the intensification of reality. Certain modern artists, such as Klee and Mondriaan, achieve pure geometric form as the ultimate truth, to them, of patterns of visual reality, once superficial appearances are penetrated. But this is an insight that is recognized in the work of archaic man as artist and in many artistic traditions. Michael Sullivan speaks of the way in which Chinese painters spent years wandering among the hills " in a world in which visual and psychical experiences are inextricably interwoven." He continues:

> Such experiences can find expression only in a language that is both visual and abstract – visual enough so that the forms that give rise to it may be apprehended, conveyed, and recognized for what they are, yet abstract enough to convey upon the forms thus created the validity of a general eternal truth.[22]

For a second thing, art as discovery reflects the tension of polarity. It may be the polarity of freedom and form, or of spirit and nature, or of divine essence and human need, or still others. Is art from the subject? or the object? It has been pointed out that the constructive eye is determinative of what appears in the work of art, the revelation from within. Yet from the early days of a magical and mythical approach to the world to the present, the object has been the necessary food of art – the object seen, not as immediate reality but as living form. Thus understood, art is an imaginative penetration into the nature of things. In thus linking subject and object, the sensuous and the intelligible, art is preeminently a symbolic form.

A third thing to be said of art as discovery rests on the fact that artistic truth depends not on contradiction but on inexpressiveness or expressiveness. Susanne Langer discusses in her *Philosophy in a New Key* the difference between *discursive* and *presentational* forms. Under the rule of reason, discursive logic has its well-developed canons for sound thinking. She insists that *visual forms are not discursive*. They present their constituents simultaneously, not successively. The elements of a picture, for instance, have no significance by themselves. Cut a picture into bits: the pattern is lost, the meaning is gone. But there is in a masterpiece of art an almost transcendent reality when seen in its totality and apprehended in the depths of its meaning. This is a presentational and not a discursive meaning, however, to use Susanne Langer's terminology. Artistic truth (or falsity) is not a matter for verbal argument but for judgment on adequacy and expressiveness.

Religion and Symbolic Forms

At no point is the universality of symbolic forms more in evidence than in religion. Religion indeed is indelibly linked with myth, with language, with art. Thus for language it uses the human language that has developed out of man's encounter with reality. The roots of religion are to be traced to the mythical consciousness, whatever exalted heights of revelation may be achieved.[23] And there has been the closest association between art and religion: in the West, for instance, remove religious substance from this culture – the architecture, the painting, the music, the drama, and other art expressions – and one sees how true it is that the church's forms have been created by culture, as its religious substance has made culture possible.

The massive cultural expressions of myth, language, and art have had two sources. One has been experience based on the human response that is possible to a rational self. Another source has been the depths of the unconscious. Cassirer's analysis of the symbolic forms of myth, language, and art show that they come from the meeting of image and symbol. Charles Hendel in his Introduction to *The Philosophy of Symbolic*

Forms shows the interdependence of image and symbol for the phenomena of culture:

> Cassirer does not mean that we are to dispense with images and substitute instead " symbols." Both image and symbol are necessary to understanding. Both have a role in the symbolizing function. They are distinct . . . and the difference is precisely that between " passive images " of something given and " symbols " created by the intellect itself. Images are given but symbols are made. Made of what? Of the images, the content of perception and experience. The intellect takes images and makes them serve as symbols.[24]

But what of religion as symbolic form? It is universal in occurrence as are myth, language, and art. Yet does not religion mean a totally different dimension of experience? King Solomon put the matter in these words: " But will God indeed dwell on the earth? Behold, heaven and the highest heaven cannot contain thee; how much less this house which I have built! " (I Kings 8:27). Abraham J. Heschel puts it in a succinct way: " If God is a symbol, He is a fiction." [25] For here is not a reality but Reality, as understood by religious faith and as apprehended by religious experience. How can the " wholly other," the Eternal, the Infinite, the Unconditioned, be related to the experience of finite beings? How can there be any comparison between the unfolding of symbolic forms of myth, language, and art in the experience of man, and the revelation of the One high and lifted up, the Most High, the Father of lights in whom is no shadow of turning?

Yet for many of this generation, religious symbols of the past seem empty of meaning. Reference has been made to the three stages of human thought on religion as described by Comte, which, after the theological and metaphysical levels, came to positivism with a relegation of the two earlier levels to outworn theories and useless superstitions. For the positivist, religion seems to belong to the solitude of the desert, the dried-up place where life has ended.

The forms of modern living and the patterns of present-day thought challenge many traditional religious practices and beliefs. Early man lived in close contact with the realities of nature. The objective world was immediately at hand. At every moment he was aware of his interrelationships with that world. In contrast, the urban dweller now is unaware that stars are shining and finds his food at supermarkets so huge that they obscure the realities of planting and growth and reaping.

In less sophisticated times there were rich resources for emotional living and participation – in dance, seasonal festivals, renewal of clan ties with the living and with the ancestors of long generations past. For modern man, emotional life is threatened with atrophy, except for spectator sports, and his preoccupation tends to be with technologies and ever-increasing masses of intellectual information. Siegfried Giedion observes that modern man's "emotional apparatus has shrunk to a mere appendage, quite unable to absorb and humanize the knowledge accumulated by his brain. He stands alone."[26]

For archaic man, there was no sharp line between the sacred and the secular. He had a strong sense of the sacred in places set aside for his worship; stepping over that threshold meant entering into another realm than ordinary space, even though continuous with it. So with time: there were special days for observing the unique significance of the season. The New Year in many cultures was a time of beginning again, and in this season the world was, to the believer, literally made over again. Rites, carefully performed, gave him the assurance that he was doing all possible with body and spirit to come into harmonious relations with forces on which he was ultimately dependent.

It was said at the outset of this section on religion and symbolic forms that "images are given but symbols are made." To the mythical consciousness, the dancer who appears in the mask of the god is transformed into him. The name of the god is the divine reality itself. The religious object, carefully wrought, is alive with divine power, and one touches the ark only with great danger. But a crisis comes to such mythical thinking. It is expressed with fine scorn in the prophets of the Old Testament, for one example. " Who hath formed a god, or molten a graven image that is profitable for nothing? " asks Isaiah (Isa. 44:10 ff.). Cassirer points out the significance of the transformation that took place under the prophetic consciousness:

> The entire ethical-religious pathos of the Prophets is concentrated in this one point. It rests on the power and certainty of the religious will that lives in the Prophets – of a will that drives them beyond all intuition of the given, the merely existent. . . . The Prophetic world is visible only in the religious idea and can be encompassed in no mere image which is oriented solely toward the sensuous present and remains confined within it.[27]

He continues in saying that the image world of myth is recognized as something merely outward and material and " since in the basic Prophetic view there can be no relation between man and God other than the spiritual-ethical relation between the I and the Thou, everything that does not belong to this relation now loses its religious value." [28]

There have been recurrent periods in Christian history when the hunger for the purity of a direct I-thou relation between man and the Eternal has led to iconoclasm. Thus the Synod of Elvira, about A.D. 306, forbade images in churches " lest that which is worshipped and venerated be depicted on the walls." There were successive movements of throwing out images through the centuries. The Cistercians banished paintings and carvings from their chapels and forbade crosses of other than plain wood. In the Reformation, there was a wholesale discarding of images and a cleansing and simplification of drama and ritual, carried to the ultimate in the Quaker meeting – which is itself symbolic!

The matter of religious symbolism is complex, even within the confines of one tradition, the Judeo-Christian. The Bible is replete with symbolic expression – in its metaphors, its style of rhetoric, its content — despite the proscription of any graven image. The early church brought into its life and sacramental worship many rituals, objects, and features from the background of the Mediterranean world — water, bread, wine, oil, symbols of the fish, dove, tree, and so on. These became part of the forms given to the transfiguring conviction that Jesus Christ was "the image of the invisible God." But the assertion that the ultimate is expressed in a human image brings together two things between which there is an eternal disparity — except to the eye of faith in Christ as the concrete expression of the eternal. Religion is a symbolic form of a very special sort, as it must be to relate the ground of all being to mortal existence. Only symbol and myth fit the search for apprehension of Creation and Last Things, since they necessarily transcend human understanding. Abraham Heschel has said: "The whole history of religion is filled with the struggle between the pursuit of idols and the worship of Him Whose name is ineffable; *between symbolic knowledge and metasymbolic understanding;* between employing symbols *as means* and accepting them *as ends.*" [29]

Religious symbols can be indispensable aids when used as living means for the apprehension of meaning that transcends the limits of the phenomenal world. But the symbolic expression that may have power for modern man in his distinctive needs of mind, spirit, and total self may need to be those rooted in the common life, alive with the authentic realities of symbolic forms as mediated through the mythic search, the *logos* which may be found in words, the inexhaustibly expressive power of art.

Science and Symbol

The Emergence of Science. What is the place of *science* among other symbolic forms? This most recent step in man's mental development has been characterized as "the highest and most characteristic attainment of human culture." This assertion, in Cassirer's *An Essay on Man,* is confirmed by popular knowledge of the pervasive influence of scientific thought and the technological achievements based on it.

For the thought of Cassirer, science was a central and persistent feature. One of his early works, *Substance and Function,* deals with this subject. The third of the three volumes on *The Philosophy of Symbolic Forms* is devoted to ways of knowing, for which science is fundamental. And in one of his latest works before his death, *An Essay on Man,* the final chapter before his concluding summary of the book as a whole is on science. It is true that his approach to this great interest of his was guided by his Kantian understanding of experience – that the rules of human experience must be developed before statements on the nature of things. And it is true, too, that his philosophy of symbolic forms expanded from an early preoccupation with mathematics and science to embrace the broad fields of culture. This was due in part to his personal experience with the Nazi dictatorship and to the clear necessity of coming to an understanding of such forms as myth, language, art, and religion as well as science.

Meanings of the world of nature were a concern of early philosophers, as they understood that world. In ancient Babylon there were mythical interpretations of the movements of the stars, as astrology was mingled with astronomical movements of stars and planets. In old-time Chinese thought, there was emphasis on " the examination of things " as the source of knowledge. In Greek thought, Pythagoras and those who followed him regarded *number* as the key to understanding the external world; this was held to be a reality more fundamental than the four elements of earth, air, fire, and water and their constituent atoms. In the medieval ages of the West, alchemy became a persistent preoccupation and a way to search for the secrets of the transformation of nature.

Mythical views were mingled in alchemy with observation. The Celestial Smith, it was thought, completed creation, organized the world, and laid the foundations of culture. Iron was considered to be charged with sacred power. Nature had a divine dimension. Through the transmuting agent, fire, the human worker might be a collaborator with the Celestial Smith. Search might lead to the discovery of the philosopher's stone and the elixir of immortality. Man might free nature from the laws of time, speed up her deliberate processes, deliver her from thralldom to telluric processes, and lead both to the salvation of nature and of man himself.

The alchemist's mythical views on the nature of things were no key to sound knowledge, although alchemy did make some empirical discoveries that became part of chemistry. The history of science furnishes numerous illustrations of the following of clues, which proved to be false, as a key to understanding. Some tribes regard butterflies as birds – they fly. The whale is thought to be a fish – it swims. Flowers of like color are classified together, disregarding what a botanist thinks as logical relationships. But as Cassirer observes, "Scientific terms are not made at random; they follow a definite principle of classification. The creation of a systematic terminology is by no means a mere accessory feature of science; it is one of its inherent and indispensable elements." [30]

The emergence of science, as it has taken place in recent centuries of our era, has profoundly affected the outlook of man. What has eventuated has been a world of technology. But the foundation of this is a dependable way of knowing (and the Greek word for "knowing," *epistēmē,* has as root meaning "stability").

A Way of Knowing. Man has always had to take account of his objective world for his very survival. In part, primitive man had recourse to magic for uncertain or unmanageable problems, but this was only after he had put to use his very considerable degree of personal skill. These skills are still found in use among the aborigines in Australia. He can mark on the distant horizon a cloud that promises life-giving moisture. The signs read by the aborigine, invisible to anyone else, are pointer readings that are his passport to physical survival.

The signs read by the modern scientist are even more delicately obscure. But there is a quality in his interpretation that represents another dimension than that known and used by the primitive man of the desert. For his tools of observation and thought and his symbols for interpretation enable the scientist to pass from the apprehendable to the understandable. And this is possible through a special language of sign or symbol.

"Nature," it has been said, "is inexhaustible." Even from the standpoint of natural history there is ever more to be known. It is the greatest scientist who is the most ready to acknowledge the mystery of nature. Many would join Newton in his remark that he was gathering a few pebbles of knowledge on the beach of an ocean of the unknown.

The tools of symbolic expression have enabled the scientist to pass from raw observations to postulations. Thus by observation, the differing atomic weights of elements became known. But it also became evident that it was possible to project onto the periodic table still undiscovered elements. These postulates, confirmed in due course, were made by means of a comprehensive framework within the understanding.

When Democritus first sought to describe atoms, he gave the image drawn from our macrocosm. Their connection was explained by material links — hooks and eyes, balls and sockets. But science no longer speaks this common sense language. While it started with natural language, it has had to develop an artificial language of its own, one of symbols. This form of expression made possible an entirely new systematic interpretation. The scientist Polanyi speaks of the power that has come through linguistic representation and through the operation of symbols to assist the process of thought. He says: "The mathematical symbol embodies the conception of its operability, just as a bishop or knight in chess embodies the conception of the moves of which it is capable." [31] He refers to the ability to operate symbols as "an intellectual tool of boundless power."

The symbols of mathematics and science make possible an understanding of meaning in ways that go beyond even the most refined observation. Development of understanding of incommensurate lengths and irrational numbers makes possible the taking into account the fact that events are a continuum in a way that discrete numbers cannot.

Each symbolic form has its own distinctive characteristic. Science seems to be in greatest contrast with the other four that have been briefly presented here. By popular thought the scientist is a person of complete objectivity. Thus in a novel that was widely read, *Arrowsmith* by Sinclair Lewis, a physician on a tropical island where a severe epidemic broke out proposed an island-wide experiment – half the persons to get a certain treatment which might cure them, the other half to be left without the treatment, as a control group.

A different picture is drawn in *Personal Knowledge*. The author, Michael Polanyi, speaks of the discovery of objective truth as the apprehension of a rationality that commands our respect and arouses our contemplative admiration. It uses senses as clues, he continues, "but transcends this experience by embracing the vision of a reality beyond the impression of our senses, a vision which speaks for itself in guiding us to an ever deeper understanding of reality."

In these pages there has been frequent borrowing of a favorite phrase of Cassirer, the linking of the sensuous and the intelligible as the hallmark of symbolic form. This is manifestly a feature of the symbol in science, as in myth, language, religion, and art. One comment, however, is made to the effect that in modern science, observation is all but eclipsed by the problem of meaning.

In science there are modes of knowing other than those that can be expressed by number. Physics and chemistry have been the forms of science that have popularly been regarded as the model for scientific discipline. Do these disciplines not furnish the perfect pattern of exactness, certainty, and concreteness? Yet there are inherent limitations to the almost all-powerful attributes these sciences are supposed to have. Consider a machine such as a clock: diagram its structure and digest its chemical constitution with complete thoroughness.

Yet its prime meaning as a timepiece will not be disclosed by physics and chemistry alone.

It is even more dramatically so with living things. There are realities about the wholeness of the organism, whether plant or animal or man, not to be compressed into any mathematical formula or manifested in mechanical conceptions. The human form, for instance, has vegetative aspects. It also has capacities for active perception. But its meaning embraces "commitments entered on intelligently and with universal intent," in a phrase of Michael Polanyi's.

Scientific symbolism has proven its unique power in analysis, in leading to general laws about the world of nature and in some degree about the world of living relationships. This symbolism needs to be seen in relation to other symbolic forms that are modes of symbolic communication open to experience and a clue to what Heschel calls "metasymbolic understanding."

Chapter V

Archetypes and Symbols

The philosophy of symbolic forms gives a setting and interpretation for the creative achievements of the human spirit. Man's unique potential for symbolic transformation becomes embodied in culture. Each symbolic form, whether myth, language, art, religion, or science, has its distinctive characteristic. And however varied these forms and the many cultural expressions of mankind, there still can be discerned a "unity in the manifold." This unity is manifested by the creative act of the human spirit. The transformations wrought by this distinctive human capacity leads to the created forms of culture. In the view of those who have sought to penetrate the significance of symbolic form, this is a key both to the understanding of the riddle of man himself and a means of glimpsing images of reality.

Universalizing Forces in Culture

Two observations may be made on present-day meanings of "culture." One is the obvious fact that in our world all existing cultures have perforce entered actively into the stream of human history. Western culture, which a few decades earlier was inclined to be regarded (by Westerners) as pattern and model, is now seen to be but one twig of a tree whose branches derive from a single trunk. A second observation is that, instead of a sense of high pride in the achievements of "advanced" culture, there is an active sense of questioning the future of mankind. One need not accept a prophecy of inescapable doom, such as is found in Spengler's *Decline of the West,* to be aware of being between disasters that have happened and others still to come.

In a book with the significant title *The Springs of Creativity,* H. Westman gives effective expression to the threat of dark forces that are as truly present for us as any known by primitive man. He says:

> As surely as primitive man feels himself to be, and is, at the mercy of nature, both inner and outer, we feel ourselves to be at the mercy of our own inventions and social organizations and of still darker forces equally if not more powerful than any we imagine we control by science. We think we have no choice and that therefore we have no responsibility. But the bomb, hovering, about to drop, is an exact correlative of a portion of our own deepest nature, and it is there so ominously and so obviously because we have chosen not to look and not to listen to the irrational and the illogical, the numinous and the dark. . . .[1]

This author raises the insistent question of how man is to find wholeness (which has root meanings in "hale" and "holy"). The answer will not come through any partial selfhood, he points out. At a deeper level of personality than can be found in any social organization that seems to promise security, we must and will have a symbolic order "that promises to deal with the *whole* of our experience and with all our needs."[2]

What the psychologist and the student of history and society see now so plainly has been set forth through the ages in the images of poets, artists, and other seers. Reference has been made to the Greek plays centered on Oedipus, and the meanings of his crime of slaying his father Laius and unwittingly marrying his mother Jocasta. There is a memorable passage in Gilbert Murray's translation of the original play. A messenger comes bearing the news of Oedipus' blinding himself in an act of contrition and unbearable sense of guilt; to destroy his own eyes he uses a gold pin torn from the breast of his mother's garment, saying:

> Out! Out! Ye never more shall see
> Me nor the anguish nor the sins of me,
> Ye looked on lives whose like the earth never bore,
> Ye knew not those my spirit thirsted for:
> Therefore be dark forever.

The names of the son and the father, Oedipus and Laius, mean respectively the sun and darkness. The slaying of darkness was attended by the most tragic circumstances, as portrayed by that dramatist. The self-destruction by Oedipus of his own organs of vision is a metaphor for the painful difficulty of relating selfhood and consciousness to the organic vitalities of nature.

The same theme has been used by one after another of the great figures of literature. Goethe's *Faust* described with acute feeling the two souls lodged within his breast, "which struggle there for undivided reign." In *Billy Budd*, Herman Melville describes the disappearance into the vortex of the body of one whose innocence was symbolized by the whiteness of the hammock that became his shroud. In the Biblical story of the slaying of Abel by his brother Cain, the murderer is marked with a sign on his forehead. This guarantees that he does not die, blindly driven by the forces of nature, until the theme is further explored in the light of man's freedom of choice.

This aspect of the human self, from all evidence, has been little changed since Paleolithic times. What, of course, has been changed is the enormous accretion of intellectual knowledge. And particularly in the Western world, there has been established the ideal of the rational man and the conviction that the mark of the ideal individual is to come as close as possible to the supposed complete objectivity of the scientist.

In the book by H. Westman, referred to above, the author attributes many distresses of this century to the image expressed in the familiar formula of Descartes: "I think, therefore I am." In one form or another the presuppositions of this formula have been of overweening importance in the life of Western man for the last century or two. Its continuing power is manifested in the predominant emphases of modern education, what has been significantly termed "the knowledge industry." Techniques are perfected for adding more efficiently to the acquisition of ever more knowledge—faster reading, use of teaching machines, audio-visual aids, and so on. All of this has been done with only a minimum of concern for the modern meanings of the ancient dictum, "Know thyself."

Mr. Westman describes his confrontation of a patient, a highly intellectual business executive, with a passage from C. G. Jung, which had in it the sense of responsibility of each individual for the cause of civilization. There were these words:

> If the great cause fails, it is because the individuals fail, because I fail. So I must first put myself right. And as authority has lost its spell, I need for this purpose knowledge and experience of the most intimate and intrinsic foundations of my subjective being, so as to build my base upon the eternal factors of the soul.[3]

What was difficult for this patient to give up, at that moment, was his trust that the science of the psyche could cure his inner malaise as efficiently as medicine copes with disease. What was supremely difficult for him to accept was what it means to be a responsible person, responsibly searching the roots of his authentic being. His ruling image was the mechanical view of all existence, of the universe as a machine, with science to explain it.

The use made of emblems and signs in totalitarian movements are ways of finding symbolic forms that seem to promise wholeness. In East Germany there are elaborate rituals for receiving young people into formal relationship to that regime, which might be called a secularized confirmation procedure. *Izvestia*, it is reported, has sponsored a contest for appropriate "Soviet rites" that would meet the yearning evident in the continuing use of church rituals for Baptism, marriage, and other human needs – even on the part of those with no real religious belief.

A key to the unconscious and its symbols is found in the archetypes, particularly for those who have been deeply influenced in their understanding and experience by the thought of Carl G. Jung. But the recognition of the interpretation of the powers of the unconscious in the wholeness of living is seen and emphasized by many who may not make extensive use of the Jungian terminology or structures of explanation of the self.

One phrase, other than that used by depth psychologists, occurs in an observation by Jacques Maritain. It is something, he asserts, that has been missed by the Freudians:

> . . . the field of the root life of those spiritual powers, the intellect and the will, the fathomless abyss of personal freedom and of the personal thirst and striving for knowledge and seeing, grasping and expressing – I should call this the preconscious in the spirit of man. For reason does not consist only of its logical tools and manifestations nor does the will consist only of its deliberate determinations. Far beneath the surface of explicit concepts and judgments, of words and expressed resolutions or movements of the will, are the sources of knowledge and poetry, of love and truly human desires, hidden in the spiritual darkness of the intimate vitality of the soul.[4]

The impact of the intellect on the world of images and emotions, Maritain adds, is "but a humble and trembling movement," yet it is an invaluable one toward an intelligible content to be grasped.

The Mythic Mode

Another way of expressing the meaning of this aspect of knowing is referred to by Cassirer as the "mythic mode." Its importance in his view is indicated by the fact that the entire second volume of *The Philosophy of Symbolic Forms* is given to "The Mythical Consciousness." The world of this consciousness, Cassirer stresses, is a dramatic world. Ritual is its motor expression and myth its epic. "The real substratum of myth" says Cassirer, "is not a substratum of thought but of feeling. . . . Its view of life is a synthetic, not an analytic one." [5]

The mythic mode was coincidental with language, up to a certain point. In that period of human thinking there was complete identity between "name" and "thing." In time the power of *logos* asserted itself in language. Symbolization was for archaic man often his most effective reach for meaning beyond the power of words. So it is with growing children, still with an elementary use of the mother tongue. So it is too for the moments in existence when it is tacitly and perhaps unconsciously recognized that any verbal expression is inadequate.

Cassirer's later writings showed a steadily increasing recognition of present-day forms of the mythical consciousness and of the unconscious. He had a profound antipathy to Freud's emphases, notably on an all-pervasive disguised sexuality. For him the generative idea was not the animal drives but the conception of the unconscious mechanism through which the libido works, manifested in the dream and in the mythmaking processes. In these he was keenly aware of the primary forms of conception that underlie discursive reason. Mrs. Langer points out that in his work on "The Mythical Consciousness" there is inherently a close link between his own new epistemology and the new psychiatry. His theme, she says, "rounds out the modern philosophical picture of human mentality to embrace psychology and anthropology and linguistics, which had broken the narrow limits of rationalist theory, in a more adequate conceptual frame." [6]

A further source of light on symbols of the unconscious, apart somewhat from the technical work of depth psychology and psychoanalysis, is the wide field of art. As pointed out in an earlier chapter, art in its human origins is no less fundamental than are myth and language and religion. The marvelous expressions found in cave paintings and extensive and masterful rock carvings of early man, even though perhaps primarily for purposes of magic, stand in mute and eloquent witness to the search for expression that transcends discursive reason.

In a description of the work of three modern artists, George W. Digby points out how forcefully modern art reveals "the psychic events which come and go unbidden." The primary purpose, he emphasizes, is not imitation or to produce a mirror image of something in nature. Rather its function is to "mirror our own hidden and lost depths and heights to ourselves." Art from such sources also reflects, Digby adds, the changes and tendencies of the times and many collective reactions still only imminent and undefined in other spheres.[7]

In art, then, there is a powerful means of understanding, through the irreplacable function of symbolic transformation, the relations of the depths of being to the surface of consciousness and to rational analyses. The wealth of understanding open through this symbolic expression is beyond any easy description. In all cultures there have been developed traditions of art expression through a broad spectrum of arts – the dance, drawing, painting, sculpture, music, architecture, and all that embodies form-giving and beauty-seeking impulses in significant manifestations. Digby interprets the meaning of the symbol in art thus:

> The symbol is no mere conventional sign which can be translated into another word or sign. It is essentially something which is not fully known. It conveys a meaning which is beyond the compass of rational mind; the awareness of many different levels of psycho-somatic being can express itself in,

> and by means of, the symbol. For the symbol speaks equally to the conscious and to the unconscious sides of men.[8]

Another way of saying this is that experience is not solely conceptual. Talk, even about a reality so dynamic as the symbol in the unconscious, does not necessarily open one to the power of that symbol. But because it is inherent in the symbol that it has the potential of breaking open the immediacy of the material and the spiritual in unbroken unity, its promise is present for those who are willing to do other than seek to manipulate from without what may be a transforming experience from within.

A term fundamental to Jungian thought of the unconscious is the "archetypes." But the term itself is a very old one. Its original use points toward Being. Augustine says of archetypes:

> They themselves do not come into being or perish but everything which does come into being or perishes is said to be formed according to them. . . . These primary things are not only ideas but are true, because they are eternal and because they remain the same and unchangeable. Through participation in them it happens that everything is what it is and how it is.[9]

Such a verbal statement may seem the most arid of intellectual formulations, however important in the history of philosophical ideas. But there is nothing of arid intellectualism in the apprehension of the power of the archetypes as viewed and experienced through depth psychology. To be sure, understanding of this reality is not easy, particularly for modern man so completely given over to a solely rational existence. His nearest experience to firsthand contact may be his dreams. But to gain insight into dreams, especially one's own, is difficult. Jung puts the matter into words — insofar as words help:

> . . . since so many people have chosen to treat archetypes as if they were part of a mechanical system that can be learned by rote, it is essential to insist that they are not mere names,

> or even philosophical concepts. They are pieces of life itself – images that are integrally connected to the living individual by the bridge of the emotions. That is why it is impossible to give an arbitrary (or universal) interpretation of any archetype. It must be explained in the manner indicated by the whole life-situation of the particular individual to whom it relates.[10]

The individual looks out on an infinity in two respects – an infinity of the cosmos and an infinity of spirit, in the unfathomable depths of selfhood. The unconscious is that part of the self that, in the Western world at least, has been so radically repressed – until the outbreaks of the new primitivism in the events of history reveal how truly irrepressible is this aspect of the self. Martin Buber uses the term "the narrow ridge" in describing the way man must traverse, and he asserts that the symbol means a covenant "between the Absolute and the concrete." It is lived concreteness that produces the symbol, and only through this concreteness can the meaning of the symbol be renewed. He says:

> All symbols are ever in danger of becoming spiritual, and not binding images, instead of remaining real signs sent into life; all sacraments are ever in danger of becoming plain experiences levelled down to the "religious" plane, instead of remaining the incarnate connection between what is above and below.

The highest manifestation of the symbol, he asserts, is in fact a human life lived in relation to the Absolute.[11]

Chapter VI

Image and Sign

In George Bernard Shaw's play *Saint Joan,* the Maid tells of her source of guidance: "I hear voices telling me what to do. They come from God." On being informed that the voices come from imagination, she replies: "Of course; that is how the messages of God come to us."

Image and sign, including symbol and metaphor, are ways in which messages from the world are conveyed to everyone. Signs are shared to some extent with the animal world; sensitivity to scent, sight, sound, and other natural signs are the condition of animal survival. Indeed some animals respond to signs that are beyond human perception, such as the sounds that dogs hear which are hypersonic for humans, or the radar-like echoes that guide flying bats and some aquatic animals such as dolphins. But to animals the world of symbol and metaphor is apparently forever closed, even though their sensitivity is accompanied by some degree of mentality.

The Image

The range of "image" is wide in its meanings. The term has come into widespread use in human relations. The *image* of a person or of an institution or corporate body can be artificially manipulated. Imagery of a sort, on the other hand, seems a part of all life — the outreach of the amoeba for food, the pattern of nest building by birds, and all that gives goal and direction to life. In the human being the tremendous activity of the psyche works into meaning the raw materials that are furnished through the stream of images, whether from external impressions or through the inner activities of the imagination.

At another extreme is the theological use of the term in the phrase "image of God." There is the most explicit Biblical statement that man, male and female, was created in the image of God (Gen. 1:27). This faith carries with it the possibility both of greatness and of weakness; as Paul Tillich observes, "Only he who is the image of God has the power of separating himself from God." [1] But according to one fundamental assertion, humanity has such possibility that on one occasion the Logos that was at the beginning of all things entered into it, and "the Word became flesh" through one who was the image of the invisible God.

The many changes in man's image of his world, which have come about through new understandings and novel ways of perceiving, have profoundly modified the signs that have meaning for man's existence, and for his interpretation of signs through living symbol and imaginative metaphor. "Images are given but symbols are made," it has been said, but since symbols are made from images, it is obvious that the relations between image, sign, symbol, and metaphor are intimately close.

One fundamental change in human mentality takes place when man moves from the typical outlook of archaic man to a developed culture. To the mythical consciousness, thought and thing are almost inseparable. This is illustrated in the power attributed to the *name* of a thing or a person. Among certain primitive peoples of today there is absolute secretiveness about the name each bears. To hold the name in memory is to hold power over the person or object. Archaic man had other difficulties in separating what seem to us clearly distinct realities, such as waking experience and the vividness of dreams, or the condition of being alive and existence after death.

Cassirer states this outlook so clearly that it is well to quote at some length this characteristic of the mythical consciousness:

> For mythical thinking all contents crowd together into a single plane of reality; everything perceived possesses as such a character of reality; the image like the word is endowed with real forces. It not only represents the thing for the subjective reflection of a third party, an observor; it is a part of its reality and efficacy. A man's image like his name is an *alter ego;* what happens to the image happens to the man himself. Thus image magic and object magic are never sharply differentiated. The instrument of magic can equally well be a man's image or a physical part of him, such as his nails or his hair. If an enemy's image is stuck by pins or pierced by arrows, he himself will suffer immediately. And it is not alone this passive efficacy that images possess. They may exert an active power, equivalent to that of the object itself. A wax model of an object is the same and acts the same as the object it represents. A man's shadow plays the same role as his image or picture. It is a real part of him and subject to injury; every injury to the shadow affects the man himself.[2]

Of the influences enabling a differentiation between *thing* and its *meaning,* one was the power of the artistic vision. In the account in an earlier chapter of the magnificent art of Cro-Magnon man, found in the cave at Lascaux and elsewhere, it was pointed out that the primary and original purpose of this art was very probably magical. Control of hunting, and its success, was a matter of life and death. Yet the detailed attention lavished by those early artists on the drawings and paintings point to a reality other than sheer identification with the object. Judging from present-day primitive men and their art, even when magic is a dominant motive, there is clearly at work an allied impulse whose origins are aesthetic creation and satisfaction.

A present-day interpretation of this impulse to image making for the satisfaction of a deep-seated desire to give external form to an inner vision is found in a description by Ladislas Segy. In his book *African Sculpture Speaks,* the writer points out that the contemporary African artist may indeed share the collective beliefs of his people in magico-religious animism. But the sculptor is also an individual. There is an urge to give body and shape of a tangible sort to the traditional figures that he carves or molds. He follows the time-honored canons of tribal tradition. Yet there flows from his tool the form he inwardly glimpses. The author of this work says:

> Animate nature whether expressed in human, animal or plant life is manifested in visible forms. To order and subjugate them to his will, man deformed them or transformed them into *invented* forms, products of his creative volition. This "will to form" . . . turned to denaturalized forms to assert man's dominance and independence, and to express his individual personality and to stamp it on his work. The forms became truly *new creations,* symbolizing man's presence on earth and his mastery over nature.[3]

What comes into being, this writer makes plain, is not an imitation of visual reality. Rather it is a bodying forth of a conceptual reality. The works of the artists do provide images. But these are images of an intuitive concept, objectifications of an emotional reality. He continues: "The emotional reality was a struggle against fear of the spirit forces. By overcoming his fear . . . [the artist] attained a feeling of superiority, controlling forces which had hitherto controlled him."[4]

There are numerous instances in the history of art that testify to the way in which the aesthetic impulse in its growing realization pointed, through the images created, to another order of reality. Thus the statues, which were designed in Egyptian burial practice to stand by the mummy as representation of the departed one and to assure a locus for his spirit, came to be invested with an artistic form that went beyond merely funerary use. An icon may, from another perspective, be appreciated as a work of art. Erich Kahler says that "ultimately the image is no longer merely a road to reality but the very figuration of reality – more than that, it is in itself a new, independent reality." [5] An image may be a sign of a traditional way of life or belief. It may also manifest a creative mastery of form. In either perspective it is a witness to a common humanity for which images have fundamental meaning. Such images are on the way from a purely physical existence, where thing and thought are virtually identified, to a mental existence, in which significant form is a pointer to a realm of reality known only through realization of inward meaning.

Form-creating forces are clearly at work even in the mythical consciousness – in the forms that mythic insights take and in the movements of the mythic through language and art to another level of image. In science there has been traced the presence of dynamic pattern at work in the single cell – downward to the atomic structure and upward to the organism. The movement from mere existence to meaning, imaged at its most exalted in religious understanding, apprehension, and experience, has at least elemental expression in the outreach of the amoeba and in the structures of matter.

The atom has a capacity to effect combinations. Astrophysics enables students of nature to see movement toward ever more complex structures of electrons and protons. It would be putting a heavy strain on intelligible language to say that the atom had any image of its potential. Yet an agelong process can be traced, which has extended over hundreds of millions of years in the earth's evolution; in this, atoms and molecules became joined in more and more complex structures of inanimate matter and were the foundation in existence of viruslike specks of living matter. Michael Polanyi, in his book *Personal Knowledge,* points to the emergence of protozoan multi-cellular organisms, and finally consciousness. He says: "Our own primeval ancestry has produced a life of the mind which claims to be guided by universal standards. By this act a prime cause emergent in time has directed itself at aims that are timeless." [6] This author continues in saying that "so far as we know, the tiny fragments of the universe embodied in man are the only centers of thought and responsibility in the visible world. If that be so, the appearance of the human mind has been so far the ultimate stage in the awakening of the world." [7]

It is in religion that there comes the illuminating differentiation between image and meaning. In the Judeo-Christian tradition there was the most explicit proscription of the making of images. Old Testament prophets poured out excoriating scorn on those who from one piece of wood fashioned an object of worship and some object of use, measured with compass and rule.

The psalmist's declaration that "the heavens declare the glory of God" might have sounded strange to his Near Eastern neighbors. To the latter the observed heavens with their celestial objects *were* gods. The Hebrew seer had made a clear and final distinction between existence and meaning; he knew that back of the visible was that reality which could be apprehended only as the transcendent. Cassirer says:

> The new ideality, the new spiritual dimension which is opened up through religion not only lends myth a new signification but actually introduces the opposition between "meaning" and "existence" into the realm of myth. Religion takes the decisive step that is essentially alien to myth; in its use of sensuous images it recognizes them as such — a means of expression which, though they reveal a determinate meaning, must necessarily remain inadequate to it, which "point" to this meaning but never wholly exhaust it.[8]

The realization of the true meaning of the true image is the aim of the master artist, as indeed it is of the worshiper in spirit and in truth. The artist confronts the natural object not to represent it but to reveal it. Paul Cézanne's landscapes transfigure the rocks and pines, not by identification and imitation but by meaning and ineffable power. In worship there may be aid given by certain figures — stained glass in meaningful patterns, the architectural form. But, as Dr. Robert Ulich has observed, "The silence of the Quakers [in worship] is one of mankind's greatest symbolic acts." [9] Its imagelessness is a virtual image of the approach to the Eternal.

The artist Ernest Fuchs has said concerning images: "For me, the world of images is one of those parables whose language, enigmatic though it is, and often hard to decipher, seek to express the inexplicable mystery of the creation and of the Creator who made the whole universe the likeness of his everlasting glory." [10]

The image of the world changes. The human need for images persists. Man responds to impressions. He responds no less to images. They do not flit by as mere momentary images. For understanding they are ways of knowing.

Sign, Symbol, Metaphor

In political elections among preliterate peoples, ways must be found to point out given candidates or political parties. In India's first General Elections in late 1951, some 105 million persons were guided in their choices by signs on the ballots. There were used printed illustrations of objects such as a hut, a lamp, a tree, an elephant, a camel, and so on. This was a vast effort on initial steps toward the use of the suffrage. But it was found that even the plainest of signs, demanding no knowledge of reading, were subject to misunderstanding.

As described by Khrishnalal Shridharani, there was the greatest difficulty in making these signs purely a system of communication. The aim was a fair and free election. But signs easily became a form of totem magic or symbols charged with powerful religious feeling. Efforts had been made to eliminate signs that had religious connotations, such as the monkey, the cow, the crescent, and so on. Despite the conscious effort to keep emotionally charged patterns away from the system of signs, the signs easily became symbols. The Congress sign of the ox, for example, was in some cases taken to stand for the sacred mount of Shiva, Nandi the Bull.

An instructive relating of sign and symbol is made by the Indian writer describing this experiment:

> A symbol suggests a wider meaning than a sign, and often releases an unconscious fulfilment of a repressed tendency. It is sometimes supposed to be a magical formula. By handling meanings and references far beyond the range of a simple sign, by becoming a substitute for direct experience, the symbol enables the human being to transcend the immediately given in their individual experience and to join in a larger common understanding that sometimes leads to humanity and sometimes to mass hysteria.[11]

Against the background of this experiment of an Indian election, the writer observes that symbols may become the greatest of human drivers, slave masters as well as inspirers, as they invoke thought and feelings and values.

Reference has been made to a term, and a practice, in ancient Greek life bearing on symbolism: the *symbola* might be a broken piece of bone, matched with one held by the priest, which admitted the acolyte to the Mysteries' rites. Another term, *semiosis*, was restricted to signs in the attempt to differentiate between sign and symbol. A modern use of agreed upon signs, which are supposed to have a direct and immediate and unmistakable communicative function, are the traffic directions for international motorists. These *glyphs* (from the Greek for a carving) are meant to be signs, pure and simple. Thus the meaning "the road narrows" is shown by putting two parallel lines, which at one end come closer together, on a triangular metal piece. These seem akin to early picture writing.

Part of the present confusion in human communications arises from failure of mutually understood signals. By the usages of some traffic signals, for example, a blinking yellow light means "proceed with caution" but in other usages it signifies "come to a full stop."

Indeed, failures of communication can occur among animals of different species. Animals of a given species have a set of built-in signals that govern courting, fighting, and so on. Thus if two turkeys fight, one can terminate the struggle by lying flat on the ground, whereupon the opponent stalks off. But peacocks have no such signal. If in captivity a peacock and a turkey fight and the latter has recourse to the lifesaving signal, the peacock still continues the attack and will kill the turkey unless they are separated.[12]

In the human world, despite a worldwide proliferation of signalling systems, there is still an appalling possibility of misunderstanding. "We fail in communication," says Charles Morris, "precisely because we live in a society caught in a pervasive reconstruction which has not progressed far enough to have found the new symbols expressive of itself and adequate to its further development." [13]

There are close relationships and distinctions between signs and symbols. A closely related symbolic manifestation is that of the *metaphor*. Along with metaphor is *simile*. A sign is a metaphor if used with an object it does not denote literally. In Shakespeare's *Romeo and Juliet* the death that comes early to the fair Juliet is said to be an untimely frost that lies on her as frost "upon the sweetest flower of all the field." In Sonnet 65, Shakespeare asks:

> O, how shall summer's honey breath hold out
> Against the wreckful siege of batt'ring days . . . ?

T. S. Eliot in *Family Reunion* has a telling expression when he observes that in a world of fugitives the one taking the opposite direction will appear to be running away.

Metaphor takes a graphic form in Chinese poetry, where the very structure of the characters of the language, ideographic and pictographic, is utlized for making alive a world of meaning. Thus, in a three-character phrase "(The) sun rises (in the) east," each of the characters has as a constituent element the character for "sun." Here the form is added to the concept of meaning in a unity that makes this language peculiarly powerful in its lyric expression of making the obscure clear through what is known, and in setting forth the eternal in the ephemeral.

Nor is metaphorical expression restricted to language. Thus when the sculptor Thorwaldsen wished to express the courage of the Swiss guards who laid down their lives in an action during the French Revolution, he carved that meaning in lasting granite in his statue of a slain lion, to be seen at Lucerne as bodied forth by his chisel from the solid wall of granite at the lake's edge.

Another instance of metaphorical expression in other than linguistic form is to be found in the use of the scarab in ancient Egypt as a means of saying that the hope of immortality is not determined by the limitations of fleshly existence. As the scarab was born from, and fed upon, the ball of dung in which the egg had been placed, so there was human hope for resurrection and immortality.

As a precious metal such as silver or gold is not necessarily most useful in its purest state of fineness but rather with a supporting alloy, so with truth that can be manifested in the metaphors which give such powerful and lasting support to truth. Martin Foss, in writing of metaphor in drama, put the matter in these words:

> [And] as prayer confesses the sinfulness of man and in confessing atones, so tragedy expresses conflict and failure, and in confessing, transcends and purifies. This can be done only by stylization which creates distance and detaches man from his bodily, sensual expedient sphere of pleasure and pain. . . . It is *Imagination* as the power of the poetic genius which extends environment to world, uses the things of nature, but widens them so that they lose their narrow appearance and grow into the distance of universal greatness. Imagination is not an arbitrary capacity of invention, it is more a power of discovery: discovery of greatness in small things, discovery of distance in nearness and narrowness, discovery of the infinite metaphorical Present in the fragmentary symbols of transitional things and events.[14]

Symbol and metaphor are signs, but they are more than mere signs. Sign, it was pointed out in the foregoing, even of the most elemental sorts, is an indication of the struggle for mental existence. The sign reflects the world of *being*. It *indicates*, whereas the symbol (with the metaphor) is from the world of *meaning* and *represents*. Signs announce their objects – the scent of a fresh trail for the wild animal or the glyph as traffic marker that warns of a narrowing roadway. But symbols lead to the conception of their objects, and may be a means not just for the discovery of truth but for the creation of truth. Cassirer differentiates between sign and symbol by saying that the former is operator, whereas the latter is designator and a vehicle for the interpretation of objects.

Symbols as a bridge between the finite spirit and the inexhaustible depths of the mysteries of the universe have their dangers. Michael Polanyi observes that "the mind which entrusts itself to the operation of symbols [used here in the sense of the mathematical symbol but bearing on the wider senses of symbolism] acquires an intellectual tool of boundless power; but its use makes the mind liable to peril the range of which also seem almost unlimited."[15] And Arnold Toynbee has pointed to the dangers of symbols too, in the sense of aspirational symbols as in nationalistic hopes. After noting that we are constantly turning symbols into idols, he says: "Today, the symbols that are most highly charged with emotion are the states among which mankind's allegiance is divided. These are the gods to which we are giving 90 per cent of our religious devotion."[16]

There is a term with unique fitness for certain religious symbols – the term "sign event" as used by Paul Tillich to refer to concrete historical happenings that are held to have revelatory significance as expressive of the nature and purpose of God. These would have no bearing on an unhistorical religion such as Hinduism – unhistorical in the sense that its cardinal beliefs do not rest on specific occurrences in history. In the context of Biblical faith, and taking due account of all that critical study shows about the origins of the record found within the Bible, the close connection between sign and event is evident, hence the fitness of the special term " sign event." [17]

The distinction between the worlds of being and of meaning as embodied in the symbol is defined in this statement: " A symbol is a visible or audible sign or emblem of some thought, emotion or experience, interpreting what can be really grasped only by the mind and imagination by something which enters into the field of observation." [18]

Chapter VII

The Productive Imagination

Imagination has been aptly characterized by Wallace Stevens as "the power of mind over the possibilities of things." It reaches simultaneously in two directions — toward sensation and understanding. Without understanding, sensations would be chaotic. Without sensation, understanding would have no content. The formative linking of sensation and understanding is the pivotal function of the imagination. The productive potential of imaginative activity is manifested by human concerns as diverse as science and the making of stories and mythic tales. Scientific imagination has proved to be as basic for science's achievements as the canons of experimentation and verification. Mythic accounts of man's serious attempts to interpret his world reveal a flowing together in these symbolic expressions of the interplay of thought and image.

For a living illustration of imaginative powers one need look no farther than the nearest child, or children, at play. The rich resources of uninhibited imagination can be seen in graphic and delightful form. A folded bit of cloth becomes a doll, or rather a playmate virtually alive, on which the playing child may lavish unending care and affection. A broken bit of board becomes an oar for a boat (also imagined) making its way toward adventure.

In no form of the child's imagination is there more eloquent expressing than in drawings and paintings. One description tells of a small girl coming from the African bush for the first time into a formal school. She was completely ignorant of the medium of instruction (French in this instance). But with a piece of chalk she found a way to express what was back of roguish, dancing eyes: A bird stealing hair from a woman walking along the road, making an involuntary contribution to a nest! The altogether delightful bit of graphic humor came not from what the child saw but from what she fancied.

The child builds a unified vision of his existence from the bundles of sensations that come to him. Th. Ribot asserts that for the child his imagination is his master faculty and is the highest form of his intellectual development at a given stage. As he plays, invents, and extends his use of the mother tongue, he meets many matters that he cannot fit into a system of abstract principles. But for matters still too difficult for understanding there may be symbolic expressions that serve admirably at a given stage. For the child, as for his elders if this capacity has not been allowed to atrophy, "the constructive imagination penetrates every part of life, whether individual or collective, speculative and radical." [1]

For primitive man, whether contemporary or archaic, the world comes alive imaginatively not alone in story and myth, but also in the dance. And this is so not only for the ecstasy of the coordinated rhythms of body and drumbeat, but also in those dances where totem animals of the people are impersonated by dancers. There is virtual identification in imagination with the forces being celebrated or invoked. Susanne Langer speaks of the dance as constituting "The Magic Circle," and says:

> The feelings of power that serve as symbols are attributed to the realities symbolized, and the world appears as a realm of potent beings.[2]

The dance creates an image of nameless and even bodiless powers, she continues, and these fill a complete, autonomous realm, a world. Men become identified with the power of that world through the ecstasy of free movement that seems to unify space and time and to create an autonomous and living reality, ". . . the first presentation of the world as a realm of mystic forces." [3]

The persistence of this imaginative urge is seen in significant form in a cultural situation that of recent years has not been hospitable to free exercise of the imagination. Among Russia's older poets is one Leonid Martynov. He has a poem about the daughter of a janitor. As reported in the press: " As the mother works in an apartment house one day, she looks through a window to the street below and sees her daughter dancing. She marvels at her beauty and grace. Dance, keep dancing, she thinks, wiping her brow, until life itself stops you." [4] The account of this poem comes in a description of Russia's " angry young poets " who scorn the government-sanctified literary formula – " indeed, they scorn the tractor and the factory, glorify love and human feeling."

The sources of the productive imagination are akin to those that underlie the human potential for symbolic transformation. Indeed, imagination, as part of the unity of sensation, intuition, and understanding, occupies a unique position of centrality. Coleridge distinguished between the primary and the secondary imagination; of the former he said: " The primary imagination I hold to be a living power and prime agent of all human perception, and as a repetition in the finite mind of the eternal act of creation in the infinite I AM." [5]

Obviously there is a differing function of the imagination when sensation operates without the abstract knowledge of a developed understanding. Both for the child and for primitive man the self is addressed to a " thou " and not to a " that." At this stage *imagery* is the natural language of the organism. The child speaks to and with things as if they were animate, and one writer has observed that " he regards them as animate because he speaks with them." In like manner for primitive man, the world of nature about him is held to be alive and powerful. The quaking aspen is addressed personally to him with an immediate message. His myths and stories personify natural forces with highly dramatic and imaginative action.

The productive imagination is no less basic for developed understanding of science. It was long before the refined study of electrons, protons, and particles that Tyndall made this observation on imagination in science:

> The kingdom of Science, then, cometh not by observation and experiment alone, but is completed by fixing the roots of observation and experiment in a region inaccessible to both and in dealing with which we are forced to fall back on the picturing power of the mind.[6]

In physics, he continued, " the experiential incessantly leads to the ultra-experiential, and that out of experience there always grows something finer than mere experience." [7]

It might be supposed that in mathematics there would be the purest form of intellection. Yet it is the greatest of mathematicians who most explicitly testify in their methods of work and their experience on the indipsensable place of imagination in mathematical achievement.

From nature itself comes one signal augmentation to man's symbolic powers. It is based on the richer concept of nature that came from early studies in biology. Charles Hendel in the Introduction to the first volume of Cassirer's *The Philosophy of Symbolic Forms* explains this particular assistance to human imagination in these words:

> In physical science man proceeds with his research and discovery by constructing a whole out of parts, thanks to the regulative Idea of the whole; but in biological research the scientists *sees* in any *individual* organism the whole actually given and as already determinative of the several distinct parts. The whole is present, in a sense, in the beginning and in the very appearances where we can identify parts.[8]

That this fact has contributed to scientific insight is no less true than that it has been of powerful aid to imagination for, as Hendel stresses,

> Here nature offers to the imagination of man that that imagination is seeking and what it demands for satisfaction. That remarkable suitability of the organic form to the imagination of man is the thing to marvel at and to explore further in this " transcendental " philosophy.[9]

And what shall be said of language and imagination? Note a group listening to such a story as the classic fairy tale *Sleeping Beauty:* From a skilled teller of tales it works a seeming magic, as old as the memory of mankind, as fresh as the fancy of today that lives anew the vividly familiar scenes. The features of the familiar story have in them much more than surface metaphors: the development of the girl who was caught between the threat of death if exposed to dangers of shedding blood from a spindle, and the overprotection of her father. The spell worked, and in her long sleep, time stopped, and the blockages to further development seemed complete in the formidable defenses of the wall of thorns that grew up around the castle where the Sleeping Beauty lay – awaiting the magic awakening touch of the prince, which meant the regaining of a lost presence.

Clearly this story, and the many classic tales that have enthralled generations without number, can be imaginatively responded to on more than one level. Its perennial appeal rests on hidden awareness of its symbolic power of being more in intention than appears on a superficial reading. So with the wide world of the literature of imagination – drama, novel, and poetry.

In an article on " The Making of a Poem," the poet C. Day Lewis emphasizes that the aim of poetry like that of science is knowledge. But it is knowledge of a particular kind.[10] This is illustrated by contrasting the botanical description of a wild daffodil with the well-known lines from Wordsworth:

> I wandered lonely as a cloud
> That floats on high o'er vales and hills,
> When all at once I saw a crowd,
> A host, of golden daffodils.

So Wordsworth felt – insofar as words can convey his feeling. He was open to the glory of seeing things as they really are – in this instance golden daffodils, ten thousand at a glance! Through his special ways of using language, through image, metaphor, and analogy, the poet penetrates to psychic depths and " transmutes through the cool heat of the imagination " his vision – sensation, understandings, imagination.

It would be difficult to overstate the function of words in such experiences, as they help retain the impressions from discrete objects and their interrelationships. But prior to the words is the experience itself, enkindled by imaginative awareness and the peculiar forms of symbolic transformation inherent in the active powers of imagination. At the same time it is to be remembered that language, " of imagination all compact," is also the cradle of abstract thought. The literature of imagination is the literature of power, but the characteristic of language that gives rise to logic and reasoning is an equally valid form of symbolic transformation.

Art is in a very particular way an occasion for the exercise of imagination. Cézanne, for example, was a painter who transformed the landscapes, which were the subjects of his paintings, through the significance of his particular vision of those landscapes. This indeed is one characterization of art: " Nature seen in the light of its significance." The artist gives sensuous form through whatever medium he is using to a peculiar insight of his own.

Imaginative power can be expressed in ways other than marble, pigments, or music. A superb manifestation of imagination is seen, for instance, in the pantomime of Marcel Marceau. To witness his portrayal of a lone passenger standing at a ship's rail, with no stage properties but his slight body and the active appeal to the imagination of the viewing audience, is to know an artistic experience of rare perfection. It is not alone the artist's capacity for minute observation. It is his ability and willingness to allow free rein to the capacity for imaginative response on the part of the audience. Howard Taubman writes thus of this achievement of M. Marceau:

> One suspects that M. Marceau deliberately enlarges his gamut of suggestion as a number runs its course. One feels that he leads his audience consciously from literalism to constantly freer fancy in a desire to stretch its responsiveness. He thus increases his audience's pleasure while opening wider opportunities for himself to expand the range of his inventions.

The reporter points out that this artist in pantomime depends little on supporting devices — words, props, or other performers. He challenges his viewers to allow their imaginations full rein. "Like all authentic artists," observes the critic, "he sweeps away constraints of habitual ways of perceiving things." [11]

That phrase on sweeping away habitual constraints on perception points to one of the central meanings of imaginative potential for symbolic transformation. There is ample evidence from studies of perception on the extent to which presuppositions determine what is seen and understood. Both sensation and understanding are subject to severe bias, and this is no less true in the supposedly objective pursuits of science than it is in the supposedly subjective pursuits of art. Braque made the observation that "sense deforms — mind forms." And a great debt is owed to artists for their special competence in *seeing* and interpreting what is seen, whatever the medium used.

It is not only mind that forms. Sensation works through tools, including that marvelous instrument, the hand. The ancient Greeks, as Rudolf Arnheim has pointed out, used one and the same word, *technē,* for both art and handicraft. To equate artist and artisan is not to degrade the former but to elevate the latter. Both were engaged in making the world of form visible, and good design can be reflected in a shoe as well as in architecture, sculpture, painting, and music. Arnheim makes available a passage from the *Anthropology* of Immanuel Kant:

> The characterization of man as a rational animal is found even in the shape and organization of his hand, his fingers, and the tips of his fingers. It is through their build and tender sensitivity that nature has equipped him, not for just one manner of handling things, but unspecifically for all of them, which is to say, nature has equipped him for the employment of reason and thereby designated the technical capacity of his species as that of a rational animal.[12]

This author asserts that "the demands and creations of the spirit have always developed from the needs of practical living, and, correspondingly, all art has developed from objects of material use to objects of spiritual use." [13] He argues that a renaissance of significant form can be aided as imaginative achievements of hand and spirit become a part of architecture, interior design, and craft work.

That imagination is the searchlight for form can be illustrated in the structures possible to humble materials. This is suggested in some of the form-giving manifestations of nature itself. John Ruskin in *Ethics of the Dust* describes what may be found in the black slime of a beaten footpath on a rainy day in the outskirts of a manufacturing town. The slime may be composed of clay, soot, a little sand, and water. These destroy reciprocally each other's nature and power. But leave this ounce of mud in perfect rest, Ruskin says, and the clay becomes a sapphire; the sand, an opal; the soot, a diamond; the water, a crystal star.[14] What nature does through external law may be achieved by the creative power of the imaginative artist, not in imitation of nature so much as in the transformation of reality.

The material of the artist may be as humble as the slime found along the city bypath, as described by Ruskin. What is of moment is the way in which sensation and understanding meet in a new creation. An instance of this is seen in the creative form given to as inert and unpromising a raw material as could well be imagined – paraffin – by a woman artist, Pat Erickson. Finding herself one Christmas as an impecunious art student with no remembrance to give a friend, she thought of molding an ordinary candle into the form of an angelic figure. Under her skilled and sensitive fingers, this inert substance (and the word "paraffin" means "without affinity") took appealing form, an object of shimmering beauty in its translucent loveliness.

In the development of culture, *logos* becomes separated from *mythos*, and the cognitive is distinguished from the emotive experience. It is clear that the image as it comes through sensation is concrete. But it is clear also that there is a characteristic of the mind which abstracts from the stream of images their meaning. What holds together these aspects of the mind is the power of the symbol. "Symbolism is culture's dissatisfaction," says Nicolas Berdyaev, "an unwillingness to remain in culture; it is a way to being."[15]

The "way to being," however, becomes for modern man an increasingly complex matter. The stream of images that confronts him brings more than dissatisfaction. To many the only appropriate term for human existence is "absurd," and there has developed in expression of this conviction a theater of the absurd. But that the final word is "absurdity" is not admitted even by those who contribute to this theater. Bertolt Brecht, for instance, has said this:

> It is not enough only to ask from the theater insights – informative images of reality. Our theater must, in addition, excite the desire to understand, must stimulate pleasure in the transformation of reality.[16]

It is in religion that imagination receives its widest meaning and its most searching tests as index to reality. For relating human capacities to infinite mysteries, the most adequate modes of expression and sources of living experience come through the symbols that develop between human response and the ground of all being. "Symbolic representation is in religion manifested in its full power and depth," asserts Cassirer, "for in a manner of speaking, the symbol hastens ahead of reality, showing it the way and clearing the path.

Symbolic representation is no mere looking back in this reality as something finished, but becomes a factor and motif in its unfolding."[17]

A revealing insight is found on the place of imagination in religion in a statement by Richard Kroner when he makes this observation: "Dogma is the peculiar transformation of the image into a notion; it substitutes thought for imagination."[18] The positive aspect of this assertion is found in these further words from this thinker:

> Not until concepts have turned into images does the real appear to the human mind. It is the peculiar function and unique virtue of the religious imagination to make the *real itself* enter the stage of our individual and personal life and address man.[19]

And this aspect of imagination brings the human being to his closest apprehension of ultimate truth. This is not to make the claim that it is within man's capacity to grasp ultimate truth. But he can have an image of the divine mystery. As Kroner puts it:

> God as he reveals himself in the Bible is not a symbol. He does not symbolize the idea of absolute truth or ultimate reality. He "images" the mystery which is hidden in those ideas, or he is this mystery as expressed by the religious imagination.[20]

Chapter VIII

The Shaping Power of Symbolic Forms

In these chapters recurrent attention has been given to the thought of Ernst Cassirer, particularly as it bears upon the specific meanings of a philosophy of symbolic forms. There have been also numerous references to other thinkers who from their own insights have expressed a fundamental basic conviction: Symbolization is the essential act of mind, and for persons the basic process of selfhood is the symbolic transformation of impressions, through understanding and experience. The quotations made from thinkers in varied fields demonstrate the fact that there are many aspects of the symbolic process, and many meanings for those who find symbolic forms the generative idea of a new age. Since Cassirer's thought is not popularly known, and since the breadth of his scholarship and depth of his spirit have contributed so distinctively to this field, there is reason to give at least brief mention to the man himself. His own career as a person and as a thinker has given unique impetus to a seminal idea and a living influence of growing power.

As told by Dimitry Gawronsky, it was in 1917 that the conception of the symbolic forms flashed on the mind of this German scholar, just as he entered a streetcar to ride home. When he reached his home a few minutes later, the whole plan of the voluminous new work was ready in his mind, in essentially the form in which it was carried out in the subsequent ten years. He was forty-three years of age at the time and had behind him a distinguished achievement in writing and university teaching. He had in the immediate background World War I, bringing to painfully sharp focus the immense human issues of thought and action reflected in European philosophy in general and in German metaphysics in particular.

Gawronsky notes in his personal recounting of the birth of this idea of symbolic forms that in 1917 one belief had been shattered to its foundation – that human reason was the decisive power in the social life of man. He says:

> When, at the beginning of the twentieth century, Georges Sorel advanced his theory that not reason but social myth was the driving power of human history, that the actions of human societies were determined not by objective truth and cool deliberation but by peculiar images, mostly born out of hatred, revulsion, contempt, and filled with strong impulses and emotions, images, which have nothing to do with truth and often represent the greatest possible falsehood – the scholars only laughed at him and paid no attention at all to his "queer" ideas. . . .[1]

Yet the extent of truth in Sorel's contentions became graphically evident in the disarray of totalitarian ideologies and the stormy pace of events, and these were background for Cassirer's theory of symbolic forms. He suddenly saw that it was not true that only the human reason opens the door that leads to the understanding of reality.

The Philosophy of Symbolic Forms had not been completed long before another portent appeared in the form of Nazi power. Cassirer left Germany, where he was rector of the University of Hamburg, lectured for two years at Oxford University in England, then went for six years to the University of Göteborg in Sweden. In 1941 he went to the U.S.A., taught at Yale University, then at Columbia University. He died suddenly at the latter place on April 13, 1945.

The Philosophy of Ernst Cassirer sets forth some personal impressions of his associates and students, revealing as the critique and description of his thought. One dominant impression is of the phenomenal width of interest and breadth of scholarly learning. Another is his aliveness to growth in still more ideas. Yet, as one comment says, he gave individual sympathy to everyone he knew.

Since art was one of the symbolic forms to which this thinker was superbly sensitive, an illustration from art might better epitomize the significance of his contribution than words. Consider the bearing of these words in description of some sculptures from the hand of Auguste Rodin. In the words of Rainer Maria Rilke:

> The beautiful group that is called *L'homme et sa pensée* is the representation of a man who kneels and with the touch of his forehead upon the stone before him awakens the silent form of the woman who remains imprisoned in the stone. . . . The work most nearly related to this is the head that musingly and silently freed itself from a block. *La Pensée* is a transcendent vision of life that rises slowly out of the heavy sleep of the stone.[2]

The stone *is* stone. But from Rodin's hand it is more. It is beauty. There is the sensuous: the hard granite. There is a rising above the sensuous in the sheer beauty of the artist's creation. This basic polarity, between the empirically existent in that solid block and the absolute idea achieved through the artist's vision, reveals the basic polarity of Being itself and illumines symbolic form not alone in art but in all that is human.

The artist's vision in enduring marble gives literal expression to the meaning of "the shaping power of symbolic form." What may be said in summary of certain points in the philosophy of symbolic forms?

For one thing, this shaping is a *process of creation.* It is not a matter of the reception of images in a passive sense. There is a human response. The eye, to use Cassirer's phrase, is a constructive eye. "Every phenomenon is a letter in the script of reality," he claims, and the reading of this script is an active and a creative process. Creative mind and created form go together in enduring polarity and in continuing process. As a script is not a mere summation of letters but is permeated by meaning – of sentences and words and as a whole, as perceived by the knowing and growing mind – so consciousness brings to the constant flux of events a unity of form. Sense data undergo symbolic transformation, as they are seized upon by the understanding and as they take on meaning given through the constructive eye of the self.

The process, a creative one, of the emergence of the symbolic forms is, asserts Cassirer, a process of progressive self-liberation. The raw materials are furnished by the world, by reality as persons encounter it. But this is not a static, once-for-all event. There is movement within each symbolic form and between them, as they form the great divisions of human culture.

It has been noted that mythical consciousness and language developed together, historically, up to a certain point. When the characteristics inherent in each asserted themselves in human experience in its development, separation into two distinctive forms took place.

Not only is there development between symbolic forms in the processes of cultural change. There also is movement within each form. Consider the imagery and metaphors of three poems widely influential in the West: Dante's *Divine Comedy,* Milton's *Paradise Lost,* T. S. Eliot's *The Waste Land.* Each is a memorable example of literary art, but each work reflects the background of its own age. *Being* is not static, and the tensions in its polarity come to expression in the ongoing movement.

The active process of creation that is evident in cultural phenomena, Cassirer maintained, issues in results that go beyond transitory individual life. In his words:

> In his symbolic forms – and they constitute what is nongenetic in his being and gifts – man has found as it were the solution to a task which his organic nature was incapable of solving. "Spirit" has accomplished what was denied to life. . . . What the individual feels, wills, and thinks does not remain

> enclosed within himself; it is objectified in his work. These works of language, poetry, plastic art, and religion become the monuments, the symbols, of recognition and remembrance of human kind. They are " more lasting than bronze "; for within them there remains not only something material; in addition there are the manifestations of a spirit — manifestation which can be freed from its material covering and awakened to new power whenever a sympathetic and sensitive soul encounters it.[3]

This active process of the constructive eye, the symbolic transformation open to spirit joined with life, does not mean an untrammeled freedom. " Knowing and taking account of necessity is the genuine process of liberation which ' spirit ' in contradistinction to ' nature ' has brought to perfection," is Cassirer's way of defining freedom, adding:

> The " freedom " which man is able to wrest for himself does not mean that he has removed himself from nature, from her being and operations. He cannot overturn or break through the organic limits which are fixed for him just as for any other living being. But within these limits, indeed by means of them, he fashions a breadth and self-sufficiency of movement which is accessible and attainable only by him.[4]

And this self-sufficiency stems from the fact that the highest spiritual activity known to consciousness is mediated by certain modes of sensory activity. The new problems that have arisen for man have required new forms of understanding — this is what Cassirer has called " the odyssey of the mind." In taking account of the different directions taken by the original imaginative power of the mind we see " the essential nature of the human spirit — for it can only disclose itself to us by shaping sensible matter." [5]

The shaping power of symbolic form is further manifested in the unity of the productive process. This phrasing is suggested by a sentence from Cassirer in his Introduction to the problem of symbolic forms. In that he is concerned with a fundamental antithesis: *intuitive* knowledge and *symbolic* knowledge. He notes that the original content of life cannot be apprehended by any form of representation; rather it is apprehended only in pure intuition. Do we seek the substance of the human spirit in its pure originality? Or do we surrender ourselves to the richness and diversity of mediate forms?

He admits at once that *human* knowledge cannot dispense with symbols and signs. This confirms the limited and finite character of the human. He puts the matter in these words:

> For it is the necessary destiny of culture that everything which it creates in its constant process of configuration and education removes us more and more from the originality of life. The more richly and energetically the human spirit engages in its formative activity, the farther this very activity seems to remove it from the primal source of its own being. More and more it appears to be imprisoned in its own creations — in the words of language, the images of myth or art, in the intellectual symbols of cognition, which cover it like a delicate and transparent but unbreachable veil.[6]

The solution, says Cassirer, is not to go back to a "paradise of pure immediacy." The way is forward. It is *through* the specific image worlds, *through* the specific symbolic forms that are the creations of culture. Our task is to understand and elucidate the basic formative principle of these creations. The negation of the symbolic forms, this thinker maintains, would be to destroy the spiritual form with which for us the essence of life proves to be bound up.

This leads to a concluding thought that bears on the idea of *unity* in the process of apprehending symbolic forms:

> If we approach spiritual life, not as the static contemplation of being, but as functions and energies of formation, we shall find certain typical and common principles of formation, diverse and dissimilar as the forms may be. If the philosophy of culture succeeds in apprehending and elucidating such basic principles, it will have fulfilled, in a new sense, its task of demonstrating the unity of the spirit as opposed to the multiplicity of its manifestions — for the clearest evidence of

> this unity is precisely that the diversity of the *products* of the human spirit, does not impair the unity of its *productive process,* but rather sustains and confirms it.[7]

We recur for illumination of this thought to the statue by Rodin, *La Pensée.* Here is an indivisible fusion of material content in the stone that shows the marks of the sculptor's chisel, and the ideal meaning in that head almost miraculously released from the heavy stone — a face alive with the purest spirituality of conception and depth of awareness. The calling forth of symbolic forms is a fusion of substance and function. A work of art, for example, is not making a copy of an objective scene. Nor is it purely a reflection of a subjective vision. It rather is a new discovery of these correlative factors.

Symbolic forms are not only a creative process and a manifestation of an indestructible unity; they are an essential of communication.

There was a steady movement in the thought of Cassirer from chief preoccupation with science and with knowledge as such to the broad concerns of the spirit of man, particularly the social and the moral. And he saw in symbolic forms the hope of man's liberation of himself through their shaping power, although his later works reflect growing awareness of the dark forces of human nature.[8]

The understanding he developed of the relations of symbols to science showed our basic dependence on an interpretive capacity transcendent to (though related with) physical facts. He notes, in *An Essay on Man,* that Einstein went back to Riemann's geometry for development of the theory of relativity, though Riemann had developed that geometry as a mere logical possibility. "What we need" asserted Cassirer, "is full freedom in the construction of the various forms of our mathematical symbolism, in order to provide physical thought with its intellectual instruments."[9] He added that while we cannot anticipate the facts, yet we can make provision for the intellectual interpretation of the facts through the power of symbolic thought.

It is significant that the relations between scientists around the world is one of the outstanding examples of a truly international community. And this community of understanding rests upon their acceptance of a common intellectual symbolism. This is a pattern of man's need to collaborate with himself in fields other than science. A philosophy of symbolic forms sets forth a universal framework, though events show the difficulty of man's enjoying the gifts of his culture. Cassirer admitted this in saying that "civilization is 'dialectical' as well as dramatic. It is no simple event, no peaceful unwinding. Instead it is an act which it is forever necessary to begin anew, and its goal is never certain." [10]

A further contribution of symbolic forms to communication is their participation not in the concrete particulars of existence, but in the light of the universal. Cassirer says:

> It is, as it were, the fundamental principle of cognition that the universal can be perceived only in the particular while the particular can be thought only in reference to the universal.[11]

This is true for cognition as such. But the philosophy of symbolic forms makes clear that cognition is only one of many forms of apprehending reality. "For each new problem," Cassirer asserts, "[the human mind] constructs a new form of understanding."

Chapter IX

Bridges to the Understanding of Modern Man: Art

One of the ways of knowing and of communication is through the forms of art. A reason for this is tersely expressed in a German saying, "What one has not drawn he has not seen" (*Was man nicht gezeichnet hat, hat man nicht gesehen*). Art means the intensification of reality, not merely its re-presentation through copying. The artist puts others in his debt by his ability to see into the depths, whether of nature or of spirit. He brings to a focus a way of seeing. The medium is varied – painting, sculpture, architecture, poetry, drama, the dance, music. The style may be representational or an abstraction, figurative or nonfigurative. To the productive imagination the world seems to offer virtually inexhaustible sources for symbolic transformation through art.

What is manifestly evidenced by the history and the fact of developing art has its parallel in man's religious quest. He is a finite being but he is capable of at least dimly conceiving the thought of infinity. He is a creature existing in time but he can faintly envisage the Eternal. Man is dependent on a world of becoming and knows his body must die, yet in religious aspiration he wants the assurance of resting on the ground of all Being. If art embodies an intensification of reality in its realization of expressive form, it is but a reflection of the religious experience of the Psalmist who exclaimed: "It is high, I cannot attain it."

The Judeo-Christian conviction is that in that prophetic

faith man confronts God as the One high and lifted up, transcendent to the world, the "wholly other." But for many contemporary men this outlook seems impossible, and it is fashionable to speak of "the death of God." The specific Christian conviction is that Jesus the Christ is the image of the invisible God. Yet many characterize this age as the post-Christian era.

The struggle for a living religious faith in our time has to be fought for in the face of powerful secularistic influences. The fascinations of this technological era tend to preempt attention and to divert thought from the perennial and basic issues of what it means to be a person. The demonstrated capacities of disciplined thought to produce what is needed for physical needs undercuts the sense of dependence. The titanic forces of an industrial society armed with techniques developed from the data of science generate conflicts within the economic order that seem to make class struggle a permanent feature of living until a classless society becomes realized. The cause of national loyalties or ideologies that leap national boundaries can become quasi-religious in their intensity and pervasiveness. The human situation becomes one of growing predicaments, foreseen in part by seers of the nineteenth century such as Kierkegaard, Berdyaev, Burkhardt, and others, but now complicated by exploding populations, the possession of nuclear energy, and an awareness of the almost uncontrollable powers hidden below the level of human consciousness.

If art can become a way of communication between the spirit of contemporary man and a living religious faith, it will be another manifestation of the unique and irreplaceable power of the symbol. There are of course many other symbolic expressions. At a given moment of history some statement may gather up insights that epitomize in words the lasting meaning of that moment. Such for Americans is the Declaration of Independence. Such for Communists is the Communist Manifesto in their view of the meaning of class struggle. Such for the ancient Hebrews was the Covenant between the Lord and his people. Such for the early church was the creed, simply characterized by Christians as the symbol. Art for this generation may become a bridge for understandings that throw light on symbolic expression in words and provide a means of encounter of lasting and unique import.

The cathedral in Coventry, England, which was built to replace the historic building destroyed by German bombers in World War II, can in a double sense illuminate the meaning of art for religion. One sense is metaphorical and is suggested on looking at the great rear wall of that modern cathedral. The wall is made of glass panels, each large panel having etched on it a figure from the history of the church. Looking *through* the glass panels, one sees the interior with its cumulative impact from the many symbols of font, windows in deep color, pulpit, and finally the altar under a great tapestry showing the figure of Christ. One can be oblivious to that altar when standing outside that rear glass wall, though it is in plain sight, if the focus of one's sight is on the art of the etched figures. But on looking through the glass the attention is focussed on the altar with its provision for the rite of the Sacrament of the Eucharist.

In another sense the whole cathedral in its architectural structure is symbolic, particularly in the inspired use of the ruins of the destroyed building as living testimony to the despair and the hope of man in a continually warring world. The despair needs no explication as one relives in imagination that night of terror. The hope is epitomized by the charred cross standing at the apse of the ruined cathedral, made from blackened timbers that fell from the roof of the old structure, standing now more eloquently than any jeweled design possibly could.

To speak of art as discovery and understanding is to keep a live awareness of likenesses with man's adventure into the ultimate in his thought, worship, and act. In religious aspirations, he is aware of living tensions between his finite self and the totality of existence as he apprehends it. And in art there is discerned at every turn the tensions of polarity. Man's nature being what it is in his amphibious existence, this tension is inescapable and is significant of what it means to be a person. Walt Whitman could express envy for the bovine placidity of cows. But to be human is to know the pull of two realms, a fact graphically described both in philosophic writings and in Biblical wisdom.

Polarity in Art and in Religion

In a chapter on "Cassirer's Placement of Art," Katherine Gilbert notes that "a symbolic form in general is an active interpreter, binding an intellectual content to a sensuous show. . . . The opposites that are reconciled by the office of the symbol are many: meaning and sensuous embodiment; the intelligible world and the world of time and change; contemplation and action; freedom and form; spirit and nature; divine essence and human need." [1]

The whole of the field of art reflects this tension, this polarity. Consider the dance. There is, on the one hand, the mechanism of the dancer's body with indeterminate possibilities of fluency of movement and grace of expression within the confines of a given space and the ineluctable law of gravity. Within the limitations of the sensuous there emerges from the portrayal of the dancer a new creation, a molding into a fluent unity of dynamic image of a presentation in whose unbroken unity space and time, muscles and dancing surface, are forgotten under the spell of perfect mastery of movement and meaning. The outer world is there. But it is transfigured in the power of the dance, as the vision of the dancer responds to laws of an inner and unseen world of that ancient art. Tension is there. But the resolution of tension under the grace of art reveals a new world that is an unbreakable unity of meaning.

Miss Gilbert notes the place of the aesthetic symbol, of which the dance is a dynamic example, in relation to the religious and the scientific symbols. The scientific sign, she observes, is arbitrary and the religious symbol may be opaque.

The aesthetic symbol, however, is symbol at its height, and Cassirer gives the fundamental reason for this in these words:

> The beautiful is essentially and necessarily symbol because and in so far as it is split within itself, because it is always and everywhere both one and double. In this split, in this attachment to the sensuous, and in the rising above the sensuous, it not only expresses the tension which runs through the world of our *consciousness*, but it reveals by this means the original and basic polarity of Being itself: the dialectic which obtains between the finite and the infinite, between the absolute idea and its representation and incorporation inside the world of the individual, of the empirically existent.[2]

There is another significant instance of polarity in art, and that is the relationship between the unique character of each artistic expression that at the same time illuminates something universal in its import. Science, as is commonly recognized, deals with general laws. While the scientist studies concrete instances, always his purpose is to arrive at a sound generalization, a natural law. Art, on the contrary, is an individual creation. No one could create a clown as depicted by Rouault, except Rouault, and it is his interpretation of this *particular* figure, of limitless pathos, that makes a given work a priceless masterpiece, participating in universal meaning.

Yet the inexhaustible meanings of the world as apprehended through art are such that there is an almost endless variety of artistic idioms and media. In our time it has come about that we have a " museum without walls," as interchange of traditions becomes physically possible with the bringing together of art products from all over the world. However different in tradition, there can be appreciation and new insight from viewers of totally different backgrounds. It is well-known that the graphic power of African carvings affected profoundly the styles of various Western artists. The prints of the Japanese master, Hokusai, brought to an unsuspecting Europe a way of envisaging nature that was previously beyond the European imagination. What is manifested in the common presence of the unique and the universal are certain "energies of formation."

There are still other aspects of polarity that pervade the meeting of feeling and form in the aesthetic passion, as pervasively as does the religious quest for a point of stillness between the finite and infinite, the temporal and the Eternal. Where is the resting place between the lush sentimentality of painters such as Rubens and Raphael and the severely mathematical abstractions of Klee or Mondriaan? What is the reality of form in relation to feeling, and feeling in relation to form?

One can easily think of somewhat parallel questions in the religious life of man: justice and love, law and gospel. It would be a fascinating pursuit to trace the relationship between feeling and form as expressed in art in varied traditions and comparable emphases in the human understanding of ethics, morality, and religion. For instance, Nicolas Berdyaev in his book on Christian ethics, *The Destiny of Man,* delineates three contrasting bases for the ethical endeavor. These are expressed as the ethics of law, the ethics of redemption, and the ethics of creativity. Much of the history of modern art, at least in the Western world, could be written around the search for the underlying reality in the encounter of form with feeling. Perhaps Susanne Langer has a resolution for this encounter in the world of art when she says that a work of art is a single, indivisible symbol, and the stream of tensions, which we know in the life of feeling, have a resolution through "perception molded by imagination."[3]

Besides the meaning of "polarity" and its tensions, both in art and in religion, there is to be discerned a further common feature: *the urge to progressive self-liberation.*

Nothing is more characteristic of the aesthetic impulse than its imperious nature, grounded in the searching attempt to realize in living form an inner vision. Reference has already been made to the struggle in present-day Soviet Russia between the "poets and the commissars" — the dynamic urge of the creative writer or other artist meeting the official ideology of socialist realism with its determination to make art subserve that ideology.

If art were but the imitation of reality, as indeed it has been at certain periods and places, this attempt to control the expression of artists would be logical. But life is process. This is true for the microscopic bit of protoplasm, the amoeba. It is so for man and his society, and indeed the widest view available to man in his view of the world and existence points to the truth glimpsed by Heraclitus – one cannot step into the same river twice.

Art has its indispensable function in the further definition of reality, if art is understood not as the copying of a static, existing reality but rather an "intensification of reality." There are varied sources of this insuppressible urge.

One is in the very nature of persons with their valuation processes. To be a person is to be a center for some system of values. The intensity with which these values are held does not prove their validity. The Nazi Storm Troopers followed the *Hakenkreuz,* Hitler's emblem, with all the devotion that is characteristic of symbolizing. An important aspect of philosophy is the study of *values,* and the relations between Being and Value. Whether values are independent of space and time is a matter of philosophical debate. What is not debatable is the intensity with which men hold to what seems of value, and in no aspect of living is this more significantly true than among those possessed of some aesthetic vision, and among those who search for Ultimate Value in their religious quest.

Another source of the intensification of reality characteristic of art is the dynamic found in the unconscious, and the boundary where it meets conscious life. Even within the supposedly objective processes of science, there are instances in great number when suddenly a solution for a difficult intellectual problem seemed to well up from below the level of conscious, cognitive activity. That this does not happen often in ordinary life may be a comment on a culture that itself is a safeguard against the *numinosum,* the sacred. What happens in the intellectual world of science happens also in the world of art — preeminently there. Many artists are aware of forces guiding their production in ways beyond conscious control. Speaking of the experiences of great artists in this matter, Erich Neumann makes this observation:

> The struggle of these great men with the powers inside them and the times outside them seems to result in a statement which transcends the artistic and symbolic reality of their creative life. In music, painting, sculpture, and poetry they penetrate to the archetypal transcendence which is the inner life of the world. . . . What speaks to us is a strange transfiguration, a breakthrough into the realm of essence.[4]

Still a further source of the intensification of reality in art is through the imagination. " Art is the morality of the imaginative life," observes John Dixon.[5] A discerning apprehension of the reality of the imagination may furnish a central clue to reality. For imagination can provide guide lines to form and to order. Form in art as in nature is concrete. But it also, under the vision of the artist, can reveal pure form; not alone the balance and symmetry of classical style but the surging realities of a Henry Moore sculpture, a Jackson Pollock painting, a novel by Zhivago. The rolling, breaking wave that comes from the deeps of the ocean may make real the pure form of a dynamic power to be guaged by a calculus not designed for static forces, and the living forms of vital art embody form that is equally alive in the torso by Phidias and the soaring insights of a Brancuşi.

Mr. Dixon comments further on the " discipline of imaginative creativity." The quest for the meaning of things, he notes, can be conducted only through the ordered forms of the works of art that condense into the symbol the sense of what things are essentially.[6] Yet these " ordered forms " are seen to be dynamic. The Book of Job, for instance, is a dramatic poem of consummate power through its structure. The structure, however, contains a powerful dynamism of the questing spirit seeking to penetrate to the meaning of the suffering of a good man. Here is a work of art which binds in an unbroken and living unity the symbolic form of language with an awareness of the *mysterium tremendum* at the heart of man's existence.

The imagination has a focal place in the progressive self-liberation that is a service of art to man's understanding of himself and his world. The term " progressive self-liberation " points toward the indispensable response that is possible to persons through symbolic transformation. But it is not to be interpreted as suggesting man is autonomous or that the values he envisages can be viewed solely as human artifacts. No testimony among those who are skilled in art is more universal than their awareness of being grasped by powers from the depths – depths of their own being, depths of reality. Persons who would find meaningless a theological phrase such as the " transcendence of God " cannot deny awareness through art of powers more than can be explained either by the capacities of the individual or the enhancement of community.

Spirit and Life

A further function of art as a bridge to the understanding of contemporary man is found in its relating of *spirit* and *life*. *Life* we think we know. We trace its emergence from the simplest forms. The record of the rocks marks off the stages of life forms in varied geological ages. In the emergence of history and human societies, there is traced the growing self-consciousness of the human person, and his expanding awareness of the physical world and an ethical structure that can be suppressed but not destroyed. In the modern age man has acquired control of almost inconceivable powers in his technology and scientific prowess. Life, yes! But what can be said of *spirit?*

Contemporary man has become skilled in evading this searching question. The fascinations of technological power, the ever-present possibilities of distraction through manufactured entertainment, the sheer strain of trying to make the burgeoning totality of an expanding world intelligible – these and other forces contribute to the sense of alienation from self and reality, and the loss of identity and selfhood.

Diagnoses of the fate of man in the modern world have been made without number. Some lead to despair. A notable example is Spengler's *The Decline of the West* (1918), the influence of which is supposed to have aided materially in Hitler's recruitment of followers in the attempt to seize control of a new order. Those who do not despair yet find it easy to agree with Karl Jaspers' conclusion: "Everywhere man has reached the limits of his past forms of existence – as if his enormous capacities had actually rendered him helpless." [7] The same author says:

> The grim, increasingly anonymous will to power of erupting totalitarianism has a single, not clearly conscious aim: to change man himself, by a total planning that includes world conquest – for nothing else would block all escape. In the *Apparat* of one absolute rule, human existence would be levelled down to mere functions.[8]

And what has all this to do with art? It might seem fatuous in the extreme to counter expressions of brute force and totalitarian might with any suggestion that art can be a bridge to the understanding of the human situation and predicament. And indeed it should be clear, in the face of the magnitude of these ultimate problems of present-day existence, that only the most radical ultimate concern is adequate. The gist of the problem, however, is one of communication: given the "revolt of the masses," the physical nearness without community, the soporific of fancies and daydreams that pour from the "factory of dreams," – the cinema, television, pulp publications, and so on – and one must ask, "How is the vitality of life to be governed and expressed in terms of meaning, of purpose, of spirit?"

To ask this is to seek the springs of authentic creativity. Of these, the whole of human experience testifies that art is one. In an earlier chapter there was a consideration of the relation between *communication* and *communion.* A poignant observation is made by H. Westman on just this point:

> When our personal relations are truly open and reciprocal, it is possible for us to experience a moment of vision, of originality, like the artist's or scientist's — a kind of communication, almost a communion, that goes far beyond what could be mediated by the senses alone . . . through it we may comprehend the essential of the other one — the *Thou* — in symbols, and achieve a new field of awareness.[9]

If this is not a merely pathetic faith, its validity rests upon the authentic and unique power of symbolic forms, on the grammar of metaphor through which the spark of awareness realized in the human being can be made a glowing light in the face of the inexhaustible meaning and mystery of the universe in which we find ourselves. And it is the bodying forth of meaning of this world that can be traced in the symbols of art, the forms of mankind that mark his response to a reality he in part discovers and in part makes.

If this is to be achieved, it is not through organic nature, indispensable though that nature is. Nor is that organic nature to be undervalued. Whatever the Platonic conviction about true reality as the essence of ideas, the Biblical insight was the indivisible unity of the person. It is this indivisible unity that is realized in feeling and form, in subject and object, in the linking of sensation, imagination and intuition, and understanding. "Unity" may not mean harmony in the sense of smooth beauty; reality may be apprehended more in what Goethe called "significant roughness" than in the pleasant.

Reference has been made earlier to the new reality that comes into being in a work of art. In a painting the material of pigment, canvas, and frame becomes virtually priceless in a masterpiece. Shakespeare's *King Lear* rests on black marks on white paper, but an inspired performance confronts one with truths of human passions and relations, of an almost transcendent power. These and other achievements in culture remain to affect further generations, even though not transmitted directly through organic nature.

Art has been called by Jean Cocteau *le mystère laïc.* The meaning of the theological concept of the transcendent may leave the ordinary lay person cold. But a Van Gogh painting of the night sky with its dynamic image of the ceaseless movement and unfathomable majesty may move him to tears. "Art is a lie which makes us realize the truth," Picasso exclaimed, illustrated by the skill of the Parthenon builders in achieving the appearance of straight columns by making them slightly bowed outward. The long-ago artists of Cro-Magnon man left the cave paintings that so clearly give an instance of a distinction between a slavish imitation of nature and the deeper reality, as glimpsed by that artist who captured the truth of the instant in the reality beyond appearance.

Two novel factors lend to contemporary art unique resources for discovery and understanding. One is a new outlook, a change in the perceptions possible to the beholder's eye and mind. These changes flow from the images of our world, physical, social, and spiritual, that have come crowding into the foreground of the attention of contemporary man. The second factor is found in the modes of expression of the varied forms of arts that embody a changed vision of human existence. T. S. Eliot's *The Waste Land* is a poem that epitomizes for our time, with its pitiless images, some of the fundamentals of existence in current expressiveness, even as Dante's *Divine Comedy* did within the context of a three-story world. Picasso's painting, *Guernica,* commemorating the destruction of a Spanish village in Spain's Civil War with all its civilian population, gives indelible expression to the present-day agony of millions of Rachels weeping for slain children.

To trace the movements in the various arts as these have taken new forms in this unprecedented age is to envisage the endless possibilities of discovery and understanding by the human spirit as the unique powers of symbolic transformation flow through and are given form by the arts.

Chapter X

Emerging Patterns of New Vision

In the Spanish civil war of the mid-thirties, Fascist bombers in the employ of General Franco obliterated the town of Guernica, ancient Basque capital in Spain. The artist Pablo Picasso in a consuming indignation at this atrocity, in which for the first time women and children were systematically blown to bits by wholesale bombing from the air, went to work on a massive painting. It is titled simply *Guernica.* Its physical dimensions are huge: 11 feet 6 inches high by 25 feet 8 inches wide. Size of course says little about the import of this work. It has been called the great religious painting of our time. Paul Tillich characterizes it as a great Protestant painting because of the radicalism of the Protestant question implicit in Picasso's masterpiece.

Little can be expressed in words to describe this canvas. The colors are in severe tones of black and white and gray. Light for the scene comes not from the sun but from a naked electric light. Two animals appear in the painting. One is a horse; a spear is deeply implanted in its back, but even so the animal seems to spit defiance at such attackers whose conduct is so much lower than bestial. The bull in the painting seems to search the horizon, " For an enemy too vile to be contained in a single image," as one commentator expresses it.

But it is from the human victims that the full dimensions of the horror of Guernica are unforgettably portrayed — the dead warrior, a mother with a dead child in her arms, two other women in an extremity of anguished grief and pain and despair and gasping horror. The objects shown in the painting are of the commonest. But the artist's use of the planes in the picture, and the subtle distortion of proportions, and all that gives this work its style, suffuses the whole with a passion that is proportionate to the calamitous horror of this event and the fact of war of which it was an indescribably poignant part.

If one understands why such a creation as Picasso's *Guernica* is characterized as a great religious painting of our time, it will throw light on emerging patterns of new vision. There is, for one thing, the general matter of the style of this painting. It could never be taken as other than a modern expression. The starkness of the colors and the transfigured realism of a scene that could not be other than the living present, makes it a stark illumination of this age. The bird with open beak, shrieking to the sky, adds to the note of inexpressible horror; yet elements of hope are also in the total conception, for a defiant anticipation of ultimate victory is symbolized.

For another thing, the painting confronts the viewer with undeniable reality. It is not a pretty scene. Both the content and the style are at the farthest remove from classical conceptions of harmonious beauty. Yet no one can participate in the meaning of this painting, against the background of the contemporary world, without a recognition of its truth about man and his despair and his hope.

This end is achieved by the artist through bringing to bear a force of almost transcendent power, in his passionate indignation at this historical happening of April 29, 1937, expressed through pigments and canvas and the depiction of the materials of everyday experience. Roland Penrose in his life of Picasso makes this observation: "It is only when the widest commonplace is inspired with the intensest passion that a great work of art, transcending all schools and categories, is born; and being born lives immortally."[1]

This particular comment, and the meaning of *Guernica*, may well introduce further thought on emerging patterns of new vision. As this painting is a frank looking in the face of the starkest realities of present-day human existence, yet with hope still alive, so is the form of the religious vision of this age. As the materials of this painting were those of the secular world, in the content and the style, permeated by a deathless conviction that victory is not finally with brute force, so with the contemporary struggle to hold in one view the sacred and the profane aspects of existence. As the total conception of the painting penetrates to the dimension of depth rather than seeking realistic imitating of a scene, or an idealistic selection of only certain elements, so with the religious cry, "Out of the depths," in the spirit of the drama of Job and his search for God.

The arts are not the only symbols of significance for new vision. Each of the symbolic forms described in foregoing chapters have their bearing for the progressive self-liberation of the spirit of man – myth and language, religion and science, as well as art. And these are not the sole expressions of symbolic forms. Attention has been drawn to the relation between *communication* and *communion.* There are symbols of community of a very explicit sort, for example, in the whole meaning of *covenant,* whether between man and man or, as in the Judeo-Christian faith, also between man and God as the ground of community between man and man. What is being maintained here is that, through the symbols of the arts, there are emerging patterns of new vision that have meaning both for the secular existence of man and for his present-day understanding and experience of the Psalmist's meaning when he said, "The heavens declare the glory of God."

It is to furnish images of reality for a mankind in deepening predicaments that symbols hold unique promise, if they are truly with the power of authentic symbols whether of the arts or of other forms. It has been said that man is incapable of unfaith. This has been demonstrated in the evidences of the power of modern mythologies and in the substantial achievement of uncovering the work of archetypal patterns at work in the unconscious. The struggle for authentic selfhood, however, has to be made in an existence of increasing insulation from the organic world of nature and also from a living contact with an intelligible religious faith or vital community of belief. Traditional terms, such as redemption, sanctification, grace, and other affirmations of the Event of the appearance of Jesus the Christ, may lead to no living response. There is among many a profound sense of solitude, exile, and loneliness. These have been deepened by such human incidents as the trauma of Guernica and all the uncertainties confronting humanity in this age of stupendous physical power.

The artist too lives in this world. He is sensitive to its contradictions. He may know more fully than the ordinary man, because of his trained sensitivities, the traumatic horror of its violence, as well as its unplumbed potentialities for goodness, truth, and beauty. His identification with the immediacy of the world may help him to penetrate beneath its surface. His distortions may be the little lie that tells a larger truth. And his devotion to the world and its realities as he sees them is not inconsistent with the religious belief that the world is God's creation, and indeed he may have a unique capacity for illuminating the meaning of creation, natural or human, in ways that do furnish patterns of new vision.

Look briefly at some new patterns that have appeared in varied forms of the arts:

Architecture. A signal example of imaginative form is the chapel by Le Corbusier at Ronchamp, France. It was the first church by this famous architect. Of it he is reported to have said: "I have intended to create a place of silence, of prayer, of peace, of inward joy. How do I prepare myself? By participating in the feelings of others, in the unknown."

The chapel, Notre Dame du Haut, stands on the summit of a foothill in the Vosges Mountains. Difficult though it is to reach, yet it has brought many thousands of pilgrims from all over the world. The site indeed has been a place of pilgrimage since pagan times, and a succession of churches has occupied the location since the Middle Ages. One pilgrim describes the approach and the appearance of the chapel in these words:

> The chapel disappears from view as one travels through the town [of Ronchamp] and up a steep hill. During the last part of the journey, made on a footpath between banks of red earth, the chapel gradually reappears. Its billowing roof, its curiously placed random windows, its sculptural, almost brutal shapes and textures, with scarcely a straight line anywhere give it the appearance of a ship buttressed for a stormy sea. It is architecture at its most exciting, embodying the essentials: solidity, utility and delight.[2]

Reference has already been made to the new structure for the cathedral at Coventry, England, the successor to the historic building destroyed in World War II by German bombers. It is designed as not primarily an architectural achievement but as a center for the church's ministries for the large industrial city of Coventry, center for motor car manufacture. This fact, plus the retention of the bombed out building as an integral part of the total setting, makes Coventry Cathedral a symbolic expression in several dimensions. A commentator says:

> The new building is a powerful visual symbol of new life, and as such, makes a considerable impact both without and within. It was architecturally conceived as a witness to the central Christian themes of death and resurrection and reconciliation. The bomb-destroyed ruins are preserved and, as it were, out of the side of the old there grows the new.[3]

A question is raised about the appropriateness of the design used to set forth the age-old conflict between good and evil. At the entrance to the Coventry Cathedral there is shown St. Michael triumphing over a prostrate Satan. Will the figure of a "winged man dominating a horned man," asked one observer, speak to a generation in truly symbolic terms of the cosmic character of Christ's victory?

The examples of the artist at work as architect have been taken from church architecture. The availability of new materials and concepts have led to no less striking results in non-ecclesiastical architecture in the modern world, and the art is in either case concerned with bounding space. Religious architecture takes direct account of God in the desire to set off space that is in a special way sacred, though the truly religious outlook will refuse to accept a belief in a place where God is not, nor close his mind to the transcendent meaning of significant form even when it is primarily designed for the " secular " world.

Perhaps no art confronts a more exciting set of possibilities of new vision than architecture, where form and function are so obviously related and where the sensuous and the intelligible clearly are joined one to the other. Religious symbolism in architecture rests ultimately on the values that inhere in a particular definition of ultimate concern — whether these values are best realized in the plain, rectangular meeting house with clear glass windows or in the soaring magnificence of Gothic or Byzantine or modern structures conceived in the lively imagination of the trained artist who is architect.

Sculpture. Look at the work and the outlook of Henry Moore, English sculptor, as instance of emerging patterns. His human figures have recognizable shapes but, with their angularities or with holes through the trunk, are assuredly not realistic copies of anything existing — except a concept in the mind of this artist. What he wants to realize, he says, is the full meaning of three-dimensional form, particularly as seen in the human figure. Not all of his figures depart so notably from the human form. In his figures of woman in the bloom of physical magnificence are " the notions of strength and shelter, growth and renewal." A student of his sculptures has this to say of them and his achievement:

> Moore's object has been to touch us where we had not expected it; to re-establish, as he has said, the universal truths of our emotional life in terms of those " universal shapes to which everybody is subconsciously conditioned and to which

they can respond if their conscious control does not shut them off." [4]

To realize his vision he made a break with the classical tradition. Old models were shattered in search of a new spirit. He, like other sculptors engaged in similar ventures, was not in search of "beauty" but a new reality. Moore found it, for himself and for his carved figures, in an idiom of his own. For example, he discovered that the use of the hole in his human figures can have as much shape-meaning as solid mass. He was concerned with making images that spirits could inhabit – sculpture being conceived as expressing a certain spirit. Beauty? No. No more than a rhinoceros is beautiful, or a bulldog – but what strength!

One commentator on the work of Henry Moore has this penetrating characterization:

> Henry Moore believes that behind the appearance of things there is some kind of spiritual essence, a force of immanent being which is only partially revealed in actual living forms. . . . It is the business of art, therefore, to strip forms of their casual excresences, to reveal the forms which the spirit might evolve if its aims were disinterested. [5]

In his work is intense vitality. Alive in his forms are intuition and feeling, guided by intellect. The critic of Moore's work cited above says that, "Serious art is full of manifold meaning, and speaks from the unconscious in symbols which have almost unbounded fulness of reference." [6]

The conceptions of Henry Moore will test the openness of the viewer to believing that these represent either "emergent patterns" or "new vision." What is important is recognition of this artist's earnest attempt to penetrate to the reality of the character of the figure. For him, this penetration becomes possible only by distorting what appears to the eye. What he is after is inner truth. He discovers that truth, not in a smooth replica of the human form, but in what seems to be violent liberties with the structures familiar to sight and touch for the sake of a deeper truth, perhaps not yet fully visible to the sculptor and certainly not to one who does not share his creative urge and imaginative vision.

Most persons would feel more at home with the conceptions of a sculptor such as Rodin, even though these call for the most sustained act of receptiveness of the viewer to apprehend the depth of meaning embodied in Rodin's forms. His criterion can be applied to the work of Moore and all other artists of this field:

> That which is ugly in art is that which is false and artificial — that which aims at being pretty or even beautiful instead of being expressive.[7]

Painting. In no medium has art more assiduously sought to realize new vision through emergent patterns than in painting. The *fauves* started their movement in Europe in 1905, under the leadership of Henry Matisse, and in the United States the Armory show of 1913 was a pivotal point in the emergence of a new way of looking at the world and painting. Volumes without number have been given to the thought and work of this powerful movement in art — expressed not solely in painting, to be sure, but most graphically evident perhaps in that medium.

Georges Rouault, who died in 1958 at the age of 87, can be taken as an instance of an artist who became possessed with a new vision, and who consistently throughout his long life followed that vision. His work bears on emerging patterns in more ways than one. He developed a distinctive personal style, unmistakable in its expressiveness. The particular style came in part from Rouault's early apprenticeship as a worker in stained glass. Outlining most of his figures are black, heavy lines that came from the heavy leading used in stained glass windows.

It is in his subject matter, as well as style and form, that the prophetic aspect of his vision came to graphic expression.

Many of his paintings are of specifically religious subjects, especially the figure of Christ. But equally poignant are his portrayals of the humble, the dispossessed, and those judged by usual canons of morals to be hopeless sinners. These Rouault painted in much the same poses as his figures of Christ; the workman and the clown, from the commonest of common folk, had many of the lineaments of the features of Christ as he portrayed him. If one asks which is the "religious" painting – of the Christ or of the clown – the line is a faint one due to Rouault's conviction that the most humble person has "that of God" in him, and that Christ made the divine manifest in human form.

There is no muting of the perversity of the human being in his portrayals, nor any attempt to make pretty in an artificial way the stern facts of human living. The Prostitute series of his works shows in its strong lines the picture of the ugliness of corruption, as the features of the suffering Christ, so alike in style of painting, reveal the ultimate embodiment of redemptive suffering and healing love.

Perhaps no more accurate index to receptivity to "emerging patterns of new vision" could be found than in the works of Rouault, as he symbolized in unforgettable fashion the depths of love, suffering, and selfishness. Popular taste might find the style repelling and might think the kinship of appearance of the clown and the Christ repugnant. But his was a prophetic art.

Drama. The world of drama, even modern drama, is as vast as the worlds of painting, sculpture, architecture, and the other fine and popular arts. The particular approach of emerging patterns of new vision could be illustrated at length. This in fact has been done, notably in *The Theatre of Revolt,* by Robert Brustein.[8] From the background of the theater of the Western world, he traces the development of eight figures of importance: Ibsen, Strindberg, Chekhov, Shaw, Brecht, Pirandello, O'Neill, and Genet.

Before looking at *The Theatre of Revolt,* this comment from another dramatist, Jean Anouilh, bears on both the specific matter of dramatic truth and of the symbolism of this art form. One of Anouilh's characters in *La Repetition* is made to say:

> Naturalness and truth in the theater, my dear, are the most unnatural things in the world. Don't think that it suffices to find the tone of real life. . . . Life is very pretty but it has no form. The object of art is precisely to give it one, and through all possible artifices to create something that is truer than truth.[9]

The author of the book from which this is quoted observes that the phrase, "truer than truth," implies the possibility of some synthesis of reality "which may give into a more general truth beyond the scope of Realism." If this truth is not altogether clear to the intellect, the intuitive processes may realize this truth as completely as the rational.[10]

In a play by George Bernard Shaw, *Heartbreak House,* a retired sea captain is the voice of this playwright's own pessimism as he viewed his people of England in the time of World War I. The captain expostulates with a number of the younger generation who happen to be gathered in Heartbreak House. As he sees it their lives are full of nothing but romance and sentiment and snobbery. The captain speaks to them of his own experience. He had on occasion had to stand on the bridge of his ship for days in a raging typhoon. At another time he had been frozen into the Arctic ice with his ship for months on end. But he testifies that he had been happier in all these things than those of the younger generation looking for ease, for he had looked full in the face all of life's danger and horror and fear in order that he might feel to the full the life in him.

Here was Shaw's attempt to make others see what he foresaw so vividly — the dangers of shallowness. This theme is expressed in one way or another by those who seek to make the theater a theater of revolt and a means of bringing new vision. It is this that the playwright, Bertolt Brecht, is saying over and over in his plays: *learn to see*. Brecht does not attempt to do this by generating unthinking excitement. Rather his method is to induce sufficient detachment on the part of the viewers to prepare them for some inner decision. *New vision* is what authentic drama has sought to bring about in its moments of greatness, and the stage can be a platform used with memorable effect in excoriating mediocrity, compromise, cowardice, complacency, and sham.

The artist as playwright also lives in this world. Brustein, in his book cited above, notes that he lives in compromised reality — but he lives in another world as well, "the world of the imagination and there his vision is pure and absolute." He adds that the conflict between reality and the imagination is the conflict between the ethical and aesthetic views of life and is the pivot of the modern theater.

Poetry. In "Little Gidding," one of T. S. Eliot's *Four Quartets,* occurs this couplet:

> We only live, only suspire
> Consumed by either fire or fire.

There is the fire of nuclear fission and there is the fire of Pentecost; we will be consumed by one or the other. In poetry, "mother tongue of the race," men have broken through the dull routine of matter-of-fact acceptance of existence to the fiery celebration of a spirit in which feeling and rationality are fused in a luminous whole. Dante's *Divine Comedy* gathered up in one mighty effort of imagination and understanding a view of all existence for that age.

No one poet in any given cultural setting can be, as Dante was for medieval Europe, a dominant channel of expression of understanding, aspiration, and religious faith. But the ancient impulse, leaping in the pulse of the bard and stirring the mind and spirit of those who were carried along in imaginative sharing of his vision, remains as alive as ever. Poetry of this day cannot escape the stern necessity of the other arts if they are truly to "fit together" (the original meaning of the root word *ars*) the meanings of fresh and unique understandings of human existence. One of the great poets of this day, St. John Perse, reveals the sober reflection of many who must relate sensitive feeling to the demands of mind in linking the conscious and the unconscious apprehensions of reality. In his *Chronique* (translated by Robert Fitzgerald) he asks: "We pass, and engendered of no one, do we really know to what species we are advancing?" His high hope is reflected in the opening lines of this poem that recapitulates his life, when he says: "Coolness of evening on the heights, breath of the open sea on every threshold . . ."

Less hopeful is the outlook of T. S. Eliot, who in the recent past was one of the most influential poets writing in English. In *The Waste Land* Eliot's image of what men have made of their existence is reflected in part in these words:

> If there were the sound of water only
> Not the cicada
> And dry grass singing
> But sound of water over a rock
> Where the hermit-thrush sings in the pine trees
> Drip drop drip drop drop drop drop
> But there is no water [11]

The Waste Land in measured tones marks the onset of the desert-like existence of contemporary man, despite all the resources he has for distraction. Yet in the background is the recognition of an order, even if now a lost order. Indeed there is an order in the way he indicates the chaos of existence. Maud Bodkin makes this observation on *The Waste Land:*

> [When it] is compared to a symphony, a "music of ideas" it would seem that the analogy is felt for the whole movement of the poem, as we realize it schematically. In our experience of the poem, as of the symphony, there is present at any point an attitude, or set of mind and body, which involves felt reverberations from what has preceded, adjustments for what is to come — the fullness and exactness of such realization of context, depending, of course, upon the aptitude of the in-

dividual, and the attention he may have given to the grasp of this particular whole.[12]

What may be said of the peculiar power of poetry can be affirmed also of the potential wherever the word is the center of expression, whether drama, novel, or poetry, whether or not explicitly religious in reference and content. The Western world in its analytical and rational approach may have given predominance to the art of literature. There is no substitute to its function in expression, however *logos* and intuition are joined.

Music. In no form of the arts has the Christian church been more at home than in music. The classical heritage of Gregorian chant and plainsong in European life has developed into many expressive musical forms, and the range of offerings in religious music includes the magnificent forms of Bach and the astringent themes of Benjamin Britten and other modern composers. In European life there has been a wavering line between the so-called sacred versus secular music; they were joined in the motets of the thirteenth and fourteenth centuries, even as now there are experiments in the use of jazz in worship settings.

The most ancient of themes lend themselves to contemporary musical expression, as in the work *What Is Man?* with music by Ron Nelson and the libretto by Dean Samuel Miller of the Harvard Divinity School. In it hunger, doubt, faith, and loneliness are given expression in form as contemporary as space flight, when man is "riding free of earth's harness," to quote a line.

There is room in musical offerings both for the magnificence of Bach and the freedom of jazz as authentic voices of the Eternal in the medium of music. Albert Schweitzer has given a moving characterization of what he finds in Bach's music:

> In Bach's work there is something infinitely alive and infinitely clear — no technique any more but a world view, an image of existence. . . . One trembles before that power more than

> before the thinking of Kant or Hegel. . . . Bach does not seek to fit form to content; they originate together. He creates as an authentic creator. Each fugue is a world. His works are truth.[13]

What truth of emerging patterns of new vision are to be found in jazz, and what possibilities of adoption are there for the ministries of the church? Those religious leaders, who are thoroughly conversant with the rich variety of jazz in its contemporary developments and who sense its appeal for multitudes for whom the stately dignity of even Bach would have no appeal, can best foresee potentialities for religious uses of this distinctive musical idiom. The seriousness with which this adaptation is undertaken as a religious mission marks the potentialities they regard this distinctive form to have for the spirit of modern man.

The popular arts of the cinema and television exert immeasurable molding influence on the tastes of this generation, and the impact of these forms on values is in some degree commensurate with the exposure and the dynamic nature of the images which are furnished. Other forms of popular arts augment the influence of cinema and television. That positive values are potentially present in all these media is evidenced by the outstanding quality occasionally realized in what is produced for mass audiences or mass readership. There is opportunity on a wide scale for demonstrating in all these forms that "the excellent is the permanent," in the unceasing process of providing possibilities for new vision from emerging patterns of the arts.

Chapter XI

Symbols of the Transcendent and the Secular

The making of symbols furnishes a key to the understanding of the nature of man. Human history from the dawn of self-consciousness has been marked by the capacities man has for symbolic transformation. He has been formed not as a merely passive recipient of external impressions; his symbols mark his active response to existence through understanding, intuition, and all that constitutes man as the *animal symbolicum*. The symbolic forms that have eventuated furnish a key to the understanding of culture – not alone the characteristic structures that reflect the outcomes of symbolic transformation through the spirit of man but also the *process* that began with archaic man and continues as a central feature of the most sophisticated existence.

The symbol points beyond itself; the broken-off portion of a ring stood for a realm of meaning to the Greek host and guest who through it shared the unbroken unity of an experience of friendship. What do symbols, and the symbolizing experience of man, point to within the realities of man's existence as a whole?

Import of Symbolic Forms

To raise this question is to ask about relationships between the secular world and the possibilities of transcendence, and the import of the secularist outlook of many in this unprecedented age against the background of traditional dogmas of a religion of revelation. Obviously the attempt to interpret symbols of the transcendent and of the secular is absurdly impossible in any brief compass, yet since the symbol does "point beyond" as an inherent element of its meaning, some consideration must be given this aspect of symbolizing along with the description of symbolic forms.

Look at the import of the symbolic forms we have chosen to set forth, with particular reference to their bearing on relationships between the secular and the transcendent:

The mythic quest has characterized the life and thought of all peoples. There is an enormous deposit of the mythologies of mankind, as these have been recorded through extensive research. The mythical consciousness has distinctive characteristics of its own. In archaic man there is no sharp separation between the inner and the outer world, but the mythical consciousness of any age has distinctive characteristics as the meeting place of the conscious and the unconscious aspects of the mind, and as a joining of the intuitive and the rational of the human spirit.

There is permanent as well as primitive myth. The word itself has far deeper bearing than the one meaning of primitive belief that rational thought will dissolve or factual information make disappear. The power of the Communist myth of the classless society testifies to the absorbing appeal of a view of the world that goes beyond any possible empirical proof. The perennial appeal of the Biblical myth of creation reflects an awareness of dimensions of the reality that surrounds sentient man, which no accumulation of empirical fact can match. Biblical scholars, who argue for the demythologization of the message of the Bible so that modern man will not be put off by the context of the three-story view of the world that was held in Bible times, may be neglecting authentic power in irreplaceable meanings of the mythic quest.

Myth in its deepest sense is the searching quest for truth in the full power of the productive imagination, utilizing the utmost of rational knowledge in conjunction with the indeterminate depths of the self. The matter has been tersely expressed by Reinhold Niebuhr:

> Mythical terms are the most adequate symbols of reality because the reality which we experience constantly suggests a center and source of reality which not only transcends immediate experience, but also finally transcends the rational forms and categories by which we seek to apprehend and describe it.[1]

Not even the fascination of the technological conquest of the natural world can finally replace the mythic quest.

Language as symbolic form has during recent years received intensive study. The attention given to linguistic problems and to linguistic analysis is an index of the crucial importance that these have for human culture and corporate existence. The studies of language have been shared by philosophers, linguistic specialists, theologians, and many students of culture in general and the humanities in particular.

The range of possible meaning in language is a very wide one. Earliest beginnings were presumably uninflected sounds, such as are used as signs for communication between some animals – perhaps comparable to the hurrahs or groans of a stadium crowd watching the changing fortunes of an athletic contest! At an opposite extreme of depth of possible meaning are the expressions of poetry where sound, form, and meaning are linked in living unity. And the extensive libraries of the sacred books of the faiths of mankind attest the common-to-all assumption that their transcendent aims and truths can find a vehicle in the tongues of men. A striking illustration of this is the New Testament use of the colloquial Greek (*koinē*) at the time the Gospels were written. The words of these writings are of the most commonplace objects – *salt, vineyards, debt, grief,* and so on. Yet these commonplace terms became the vehicle for a message whose total meaning was completely extraordinary.

The secular use of language for communication on everyday

affairs is clear enough. One scholar has asserted that there are no imperfect languages; each functions according to the needs of the culture that uses it, and any inadequacies are met by the constant changes and modifications that are evident in all living tongues. But inherent in linguistic expression is the latent power of the *logos*. This term in the original Greek use meant both the literal word and also the underlying principle of all being. The dependence of the life of man on the living power of the word is attested by reported instances of children who, shut off from acquiring language, are condemned to subhuman existence. Amos N. Wilder asserts that, " Reality becomes a meaningful part of consciousness only through the interpretation of reality-contacts by language." [2]

Art as symbolic form, we have seen, is an irrepressible mode of expression. It also is a way of discovery, for the artist often becomes aware of being grasped by a totally unsuspected power, instanced for example in the experience of Handel while composing *The Messiah.*

We accept the universality of art as a matter of fact, and the urgent demand for its realization in expressive form as commonplace. But this imperative to express and to discover, whatever the particular medium used, points beyond itself in unique ways in timeless expression and in emerging insight. The tensions between classic forms, satisfying in their own kind of perfection, and what is called modern art can be disturbing. This is art's way of reporting that reality itself can be disturbing. The forms of modern art depart from " nature " no more radically than, say, the views of physical reality that are set before us by developing scientific disciplines. The picture given us through analyses of science of the structures and processes of nature are all but incredible in their unexpectedness and wonder. If art reflects new understandings, as a form symbolic of reality, its intuitive and imaginative insights are comparable in their import to the new vision of nature given through science in a world of accelerating change.

The depiction of man himself given in many examples of

contemporary art is given in what many judge to be absurdly bizarre forms. But the occasion for these depictions in current reality is pointed out by Peter Selz:

> These images are often frightening in their anguish. They are created by artists who are no longer satisfied with " significant form " or even the boldest acts of aesthetic expression. They are perhaps aware of the mechanized barbarism of a time which, notwithstanding Buchenwald and Hiroshima, is engaged in preparation for even greater violence in which the globe is to be the target. Or perhaps they express their rebellion against a dehumanization in which man, it seems, is to be reduced to an object of experiment.[3]

The raw materials of the media of art can be of the most commonplace — clay, pigments, stone, horsehair-and-catgut. But the presentational forms of art may set forth interpretations of reality in such power and with such penetration as to demand in characterization no less a term than *transcendent*.

Science, distinctive feature of this emerging age, has been characterized as a symbolic form, along with myth, language, and art. Here, it might seem, is an aspect of human experience that cannot point beyond itself. Is it not of the earth, earthy? Is its field not confined by the body of facts that can be established by painstaking analysis, experiment, and verification, by the cumulative adding of sure fact to fact?

It is true that science has its own canons, and that observation of these rules accounts for the discoveries which constitute fascinating insights into the secrets of nature. But *insight* is possible only because of the person of the scientist. And it is impossible for him to divorce completely his techniques from his fascination as person, even though a cardinal rule is that he must keep his intellectual tools sterile. One scientist makes this flat assertion: " Science in our time is not a book of facts or of methods but is a vision of nature." [4]

Consider the import of the processes of nature that embody movement from the simple to the complex. Let us state the outline of this process with utmost brevity. Atoms have a structure. A particular structure is determined by the number of electrons in relation to the nucleus. The simplest element, hydrogen, has one electron. The nuclei of atoms, whose electrical charge balances that of the electrons of that atom, have not been formed in a once-for-all instant. In a " young " star, hydrogen is being transmuted into helium under the high temperature of several millions of degrees of heat generated by the pressure of gravity. The process of the evolving of these nuclei is continuing in the stars of the endless galaxies. Older stars are constituted of more complex elements – the complexity being determined by the number of electrons clustered about the nuclei of the atoms. The stars that are the " red giants " may collapse, throwing out material that gets incorporated in second-generation stars.

This calls attention to a process, continually taking place, of the complex evolving from the simple. A striking statement in comment on this process is this: With the coming into being of the atom, the coming into being of man was implied.

If this vision of nature drawn from the macrocosm seems overpowering to the mind and imagination, there is evidence more immediately at hand; namely, the development of each human being from microscopic zygote to an organism of billions of cells. To borrow a description from Michael Polanyi:

> The appetitive, motoric, perceptive child is transformed into an intelligent person, reasoning with universal intent. We have here a process of maturation closely analogous to the corresponding step of anthropogenetic emergence, leading from the self-centered individuality of the animal to the responsible personhood of the thoughtful man, to the emergence of the *noosphere*.[5]

The establishing of the facts of nature is appropriate to the disciplines of science. But there is no suppressing of the vision of nature that eventuates from these disciplines. That vision indicates something more than a body of empirical fact. Something has emerged in the successive levels of these processes of nature that could not have been foreseen in the levels preceding. The molecule of water has novel characteristics compared to the two gases of oxygen and hydrogen that constitute it. And the living cell could not have been presupposed from even elaborate chains of molecules, nor could the multicelled organism, including man.

In the foregoing quotation from Michael Polanyi occurs a newly coined term, the *noosphere*. It is used by Pierre Teilhard de Chardin, notably in his *The Phenomenon of Man*. The term is drawn from the original Greek term for *mind*. Teilhard, who was an expert geologist and paleontologist, found in his intensive study of the evolutionary process a movement toward what he called the omega point. In the universe there seems to be the dispersion of energy into ever-more unavailable forms (the second law of thermodynamics), but there is discernible another process. The empirical facts of the record of life, in fossil and in living form, point to a contrary tendency. This tendency, Teilhard asserted, means organization at ever higher levels of life, leading to self, mind, and spirit. This realm of reality he called the *noosphere*.

It may be that further scientific study will bring to light facts that modify present conclusions. The proper work of science is with fact, wherever it may lead. This is expressed in the opening sentence of Wittgenstein's *Tractatus Logico-Philosophicus:* "The world is everything that is the case." But suppose one had looked at this world as it was, say, two billion years ago – what was then "the case" would have given no intimation of the potentialities that have come into realization in the interim. The symbolic form of science, with its way of discovering fact and its vision of nature in its dynamic and developing unity, points beyond. And the deep foundation of the unity of science is suggested by the dictum given for the guidance of the scientist: Never trust a fact unless it is supported by a theory.

Biblical Views of Transcendence

This recapitulation of four symbolic forms – myth, language, art, science – indicates that, while each is embedded in the secular world, still there are pointers to something other than a cultural deposit, something other than mere matter-of-fact. But it is in religious symbolism that this "something other" comes to explicit recognition. For religion has characteristics not fully shared by any other human experience. In the Judeo-Christian tradition there is the insistent emphasis: God is the holy one, high and lifted up. In this tradition there is the most intimate involvement with the gritty realities of history and the secular world. But towering above all these involvements was the sovereign fact of a covenant with the Most High.

To give illustrations of a transcendent faith from the background of the Judeo-Christian tradition is not to imply that symbols of the more-than-human are not found in other religious traditions. Abraham J. Heschel has said that: "From time immemorial man has been concerned with the question how to create a symbol of the Deity, a visible object in which its presence would be enshrined, wherein it could be met and wherein its power would be felt at all times." [6] In some religious traditions there has been a great proliferation of visible objects. Other traditions, as in the case of Islam, have stringently proscribed material forms as religious emblems. Yet in all cases there can be seen some symbolic expression of that ultimate concern which any living faith must manifest.

What seems unique in Biblical symbolism is the interrelationship between God as transcendent and the worship of God as necessarily involving the secular world.

Look first at manifestations of the approach to God as transcendent. "You shall not make for yourself a graven image" was an implicit recognition that the Most High could not be fitly approached through any object that man could make. For he was the holy one, high and lifted up. His ways were not man's ways.

It is true that earlier understandings were simple and primitive. The Lord God was pictured as walking in the Garden in the cool of the day. God was the God of that land and could be worshiped only on that particular soil, even if this meant transporting baskets of this very earth for an altar to him in places outside the boundaries of his territory. But there was under the teaching of the prophets the insight of God who was sovereign of all the earth and whose glory filled the whole earth. Ezekiel piled one metaphor on another to substantiate an imageless truth: God is the wholly other. He has "as it were the appearance of fire." He is "like the appearance of the bow that is in the cloud on the day of rain." It was one without form who "declared unto you his covenant" (Deut. 4:12-13).

That covenant became the key word in the relationship between God and his people. It was the living symbol in all that was most dear and sacred to the worshipers of the Most High. For this God was like none other. High and lifted up though he was, yet he entered into relationship with a people he had chosen out of all the earth. And his concerns were not alone with that people amid the affairs of empire. He could be reached by even the humble individual worshiper: "The Lord will keep you from all evil; he will keep your life." (Ps. 121:7.)

It is true that this vision of God as the wholly other was hard to attain. The writer of Ecclesiastes had to conclude that "the all" is vanity and that in the totality of things there is no meaning or value. And there is a fine edge of scorn in the words of Agur:

> Surely I am too stupid to be a man.
> I have not the understanding of a man.
> I have not learned wisdom,
> nor have I knowledge of the Holy One. . . .
> What is his name, and what his son's name?
> Surely you know!
>
> (Prov. 30:2-4.)

Yet a basic message of the Old Testament rests on the unshakable prophetic assurance of the transcendence of God. The heavens declare his glory. Worship is not to any manifestation of nature, not even the heavens, for God is their creator. Isaiah asks:

Who has measured the waters in the hollow of his hand
and marked off the heavens with a span?
(Isa. 40:12.)

The writer of The Book of Job puts these words into the mouth of the Lord:

Where were you when I laid the foundation of the earth?
Tell me, if you have understanding. . . .
On what were its bases sunk,
or who laid its cornerstone,
when the morning stars sang together,
and all the sons of God shouted for joy?
(Job 38:4, 6-7.)

There are human metaphors and anthropomorphisms in these expressions. But through them shines the clear conviction that the Eternal is the creator of all things and is bound to his people in the sure bonds of an everlasting covenant.

In the New Testament there is set forth a revolutionary experience. Jesus the Christ appeared as the Word of God in the flesh. He spoke of the Father of all who is to be worshiped in spirit and in truth. He spoke as never man had spoken, and made those words a commentary on what already had been deed as he moved among the common life of the people. The strength of his weakness became evident after his death on the cross and the arising of the burning conviction that the Anointed One was not held by death. He became the center of a community that knew no distinction between Jew or Gentile, male or female, bond or free. His message was carried to the Mediterranean world, and his spiritual presence in the lives of his followers manifested itself with such power that walls of partition were dissolved as the New Being took possession of what was a new community.

When Pompey fought his way into Jerusalem in 63 B.C., he forced his way into the Holy of Holies to discover for himself the secret of the transcendent faith that could nerve the arms and hearts of the Jewish people to stand against the might of imperial Rome. All he found was what was for him an empty room. When Roman emperors sought to discover the unbreakable power of the new sect of Christians, they were mystified in that the center of that power seemed to be devotion to a Galilean peasant who had been crucified. His seeming weakness proved to be the source of transcendent power among his followers. For he manifested the meaning of the Son of God, as symbolic of his relationship with God, by refusing to use power for himself, even as in the symbolic story of the temptation in the wilderness.

Along with the explicit recognition of the transcendence of God, however, there is in the Bible a radical recognition of this *saeculum,* this age and its responsibilities for man. The world came from the hand of the Creator, and it was full of opportunities for the realization of his purpose and will. Other kingdoms of the Near East had rigid sacral systems that laid the dead hand of conservative tradition on all human action. The Greeks held a view of reality as unchanging essence, manifesting itself in an enduring but finite universe. But the Hebrew understanding of a personal Creator at work in time and history was the root of dynamic action in the spirit of his people.

Man's Secular Responsibilities

A charming passage of the creation (Gen. 2:19 f.) records that the Lord God formed every beast of the field and every bird of the air, "and brought them to the man to see what he would call them." Recall the early emphasis on the near identification of name and thing; this gives weight to the expression, "whatever the man called every living creature, that was its name." To assign names was tantamount to having a genuine part in creation itself.

This radical recognition of this world as the theater for man's responsibility gave full emphasis on the *saeculum.* The world was his to subdue, not a place enchanted by uncontrollable spirits. The Exodus, Harvey Cox maintains, meant the "desacralization of politics," for the people could choose to march right out from under the hand of the supposedly sacrosanct Pharaoh whose will was absolute. The divine right of kings was washed up in the Red Sea! The Sinai Covenant, Cox further insists, meant the deconsecration of values, for here was a personal relationship of a covenant that bound the Lord God himself no less than his people.[7]

The subject of the secular in the Bible is a far ranging one. Let this passage state the point of view of A. Van Leeuwen in his *Christianity in World History:*

> Here is raised the protest against the reality of the cosmic totality, against the "sacralizing" of all being, against the supremacy of fate, against the divinizing of kings and kingdoms. Here a break is made with the everlasting cycle of nature and the timeless presentness of myth. Here history is discovered, where the covenant between the Creator and the creation, between the Lord and his people, bursts open the solid oneness of the universe. Here there is proper room for man and here is the taste of freedom. The world is now radically secularized, becomes creation moving towards regeneration, is made the arena of history, is in much pain and travail, waiting for the redemption and consummation of all things.[8]

There needs to be a sharp distinction between the *secular* and the *secularistic*. The latter is a fixed ideology, governed by the conviction that man is self-sufficient and all-sufficient. The secular, however, may be regarded as the arena for the working out of the purpose of creation, if creation is taken with religious and metaphysical seriousness, and if the world is viewed as the ground of the incarnation of will that is as much a manifestation of reality as electrons and atoms – which so far from being inert units of dead matter are known to be dynamic systems of energy.

The secularist tends to reduce man to an instrument of technological processes, to see secular forces as closed systems. No account is taken of religious values nor of reality transcendent to physical handling and physical perception. "Secularization," as defined by Charles West, is "the withdrawal of areas of thought and life from religious – and finally also from metaphysical – control, and the attempt to understand and live in these areas in the terms which they alone offer." [9] The secular, to be sure, has its own autonomy; the surgeon who does not keep his instruments sterile will pray for healing to little avail. But the discovery of what these conditions of the secular are is a way of enlarging the dimensions of the understanding of creation through the growing freedom of the creative spirit of man.

And it is at this point that the unity of the symbol may hold together the transcendent and the secular. In the etymology of the term "symbol" it has been stated that in early Greek society the word referred to the bringing together of two parts of a broken coin or ring to stand for the indivisible experience of friendly hospitality between host and guest. What it stood for was not the sum of two things. It was the unbreakable fact of the oneness of a kind of communion as friends.

It has been pointed out that symbolic forms link in living unity the sensuous and the intelligible. Preeminently does it happen in the confrontation with great art – not merely the unity of the sensuous and the intelligible, but realms of reality for which art is the unique vehicle. William Temple put the experience into these descriptive words:

> In a single impression we receive what absolutely satisfies us, and in that perfect satisfaction we ourselves are lost. Duration vanishes; the "moment eternal" is come. The great drama proceeds; the music surges through us; we are not conscious of our own existence. We are simply the subjects of a mighty experience. We hear and see; and when all is done we consider and bow the head.[10]

The reality of two things coming together as one, the essence of the symbol, may be more immediately evident in the arts than in metaphysics or theology. Reference has already been made to the way in which paint and pigment in a masterpiece become an indissoluble constituent of a reality that attests a transcendent creation. "The function of art," says William Temple, "is to reveal values by the creation of essential symbols – if by that phrase we may denote a symbol which is a perfect instance of what it symbolizes." [11]

The quest for the "perfect instance" of symbol of the transcendent has been an enduring one. For the writers of the New Testament, material was furnished by certain historical events. As A. C. Bridge observes, "such events were . . . typical of the new age, and knowledge of them constituted the characteristic experience of the new creature who was, himself, a coming together in symbolic union of the Spirit of God and the flesh of man. In other words, for the New Testament, a symbol was not merely the sum of two old things, but rather one newly created thing." [12] The reality of this unity goes beyond intellectual definitions, important as these are, just as the reality of the art masterpiece goes beyond the parts into which it might be dissected.

From the standpoint of the Christian faith, the perfect instance of an unbreakable unity was found in the Word made flesh, in the image of God perfectly expressed in one who was the "image of the invisible God."

Nietzsche announced the death of God in his *Thus Spake Zarathustra,* and present-day thought has had to struggle for a meaningful content to that three-letter word, with the disappearance of a three-story universe and all that was the ideational context of those who wrote the Bible. Perhaps a discerning realization of living symbols may furnish in the midst of time the timeless experience of images of reality, linking secular and transcendent.

Notes

Chapter I. The Symbol: Organ of the Human

1. William D. McElroy and Bentley Glass, eds., *Light and Life* (Johns Hopkins University Press, 1961), p. 817.
2. Pierre Teilhard de Chardin, *The Phenomenon of Man* (Harper & Brothers, 1959), p. 31.
3. Ernst Cassirer, *An Essay on Man* (Doubleday & Co., Inc., Anchor Books, 1953), p. 43. (Original copyright, 1944.)
4. Susanne Langer, *Philosophy in a New Key* (Pelican Books, 1948), p. 33. (Original copyright, 1942.)
5. Ernst Cassirer, *The Philosophy of Symbolic Forms,* Vol. I (Yale University Press, 1953), p. 111. (Original copyright, 1923.) Quotations are reprinted with permission of the publisher.
6. Jolande Jacobi, *Psychology of C. G. Jung* (Yale University Press, 6th ed., 1962), p. 93.
7. *Ibid.*, p. 145.
8. Langer, *op. cit.*, p. 33.

Chapter II. Protean Change and Persistent Symbolizing

1. Mircea Eliade, *Myths, Dreams, and Mysteries* (London: Harvill Press, 1960), p. 245.
2. See F. S. C. Northrop, *The Meeting of East and West* (The Macmillan Company, 1946).
3. Cassirer, *An Essay on Man,* p. 86.
4. Alexander Solzhenitsyn's *One Day in the Life of Ivan Denisovich* (E. P. Dutton & Company, Inc., 1963).
5. Published in translation, *The New Leader,* Jan. 18, 1965.

6. Michael Polanyi, *Personal Knowledge* (The University of Chicago Press, 1958), p. 133.

7. Dorothy D. Lee, *Symbols and Values* (Harper & Brothers, 1954), p. 79.

8. See Karl Jaspers, *The Future of Mankind* (The University of Chicago Press, 1961).

9. Ernst Cassirer, *The Logic of the Humanities* (Yale University Press, 1961), p. 190.

10. Cassirer, *The Philosophy of Symbolic Forms,* Vol. I, p. 107.

11. Teilhard de Chardin, *op. cit.*

Chapter III. Communication and Communion

1. *The Listener,* Mar. 11, 1965.

2. Charles W. Morris, *Foundations of the Theory of Signs,* Vol. I, No. 2 (The University of Chicago Press, 1938), p. 242.

3. Alfred North Whitehead, *Symbolism, Its Meaning and Effect* (The Macmillan Company, 1927), p. 62.

4. Allen Tate, *The Man of Letters in the Modern World* (Charles Scribner's Sons, 1936), p. 18.

5. *The New York Times,* Feb. 7, 1962.

6. Polanyi, *op. cit.,* p. 135.

7. In a statement given at St. Paul's School, 1956.

8. See *A Dictionary of Symbols,* ed. by J. A. Cirlot (London: Routledge & Kegan Paul, 1962).

9. Karl Jaspers, *Truth and Symbol* (Twayne Publishers, 1959), p. 17.

10. Cassirer, *The Philosophy of Symbolic Forms,* Vol. II, p. 240.

Chapter IV. Forms of Culture

1. R. G. H. Siu, *The Tao of Science* (John Wiley & Sons, Inc., 1958), p. 3.

2. Edith Hamilton, *The Greek Way,* p. 148. Copyright 1930, 1943, by W. W. Norton & Company, Inc. Copyright renewed 1958 by Edith Hamilton. Quotations are reprinted with permission of the publisher.

3. Ernst Cassirer, *The Myth of the State* (Yale University Press, 1946), p. 282.

4. *Ibid.*, p. 280.

5. Eugene W. Bewkes, ed., *The Nature of Religious Experience*, Ch. 6, "The Truth in Myths" by Reinhold Niebuhr (Harper & Brothers, 1937).

6. Cassirer, *The Philosophy of Symbolic Forms*, Vol. II, p. 179.

7. *Ibid.*, p. 39.

8. Clyde Kluckhohn, "Myths and Rituals: A General Theory," *Harvard Theological Review*, Vol. XXXV, pp. 45–79.

9. Paul Schilpp, ed., *The Philosophy of Ernst Cassirer* (Tudor Publishing Co., 1949), pp. 361 ff.

10. Cassirer, *The Philosophy of Symbolic Forms*, Vol. II, p. 260.

11. Laurens Van der Post, *The Heart of the Hunter* (William Morrow and Company, Inc., 1961), p. 170.

12. Euripides, *Iphigenia in Tauris*, tr. by Gilbert-Murray in *Ten Greek Plays* (Oxford University Press, Inc., 1941), p. 279. Quotations are reprinted with permission of the publisher.

13. Helen Keller, *The Story of My Life* (Doubleday, Doran & Co., 1936), pp. 23 f. (Original copyright, 1902.)

14. Cassirer, *The Myth of the State*, p. 284.

15. Martin Foss, *Symbol and Metaphor* (Princeton University Press, 1949), p. 120.

16. See Schilpp, ed., *op. cit.*, p. 344.

17. Cassirer, *The Philosophy of Symbolic Forms*, Vol. II, pp. 25 f.

18. Georges Bataille, *Prehistoric Painting* (Skira, undated), p. 115.

19. See *The New York Times*, July 21, 1963.

20. Robert Redfield, ed., *Aspects of Primitive Art* (New York Museum of Primitive Art, 1960), p. 43.

21. Robert Raynolds, *The Choice to Love* (Harper & Brothers, 1959), p. 112.

22. Michael Sullivan, *The Birth of Landscape Painting in China* (University of California Press, 1962), p. 2.

23. See, e.g., Gilbert Murray's *Five Stages of Greek Religion* (Oxford, The Clarendon Press, 1925).

24. Cassirer, *The Philosophy of Symbolic Forms*, Vol. I, p. 50.

25. F. Ernest Johnson, ed., *Religious Symbolism* (Harper & Brothers, 1955), p. 78.

26. Siegfried Giedion, *The Eternal Present* (Pantheon Books,

Bollingen Series XXXV, 1962), p. 80.

27. Cassirer, *The Philosophy of Symbolic Forms,* Vol. II, p. 240.
28. *Ibid.*
29. Johnson, *op. cit.,* p. 77.
30. Cassirer, *An Essay on Man,* p. 264.
31. Polanyi, *op. cit.,* p. 85.

Chapter V. Archetypes and Symbols

1. H. Westman, *The Springs of Creativity* (Atheneum Press, 1961), p. 16.
2. *Ibid.,* p. 17.
3. *Ibid.,* p. 3.
4. Jacques Maritain, *Education at the Crossroads* (Yale University Press, 1943), p. 40.
5. Cassirer, *An Essay on Man,* p. 108.
6. Schilpp, ed., *op. cit.,* p. 399.
7. George W. Digby, *Meaning and Symbol in Three Modern Artists* (London: Faber & Faber, Ltd.), p. 18.
8. *Ibid.,* p. 22.
9. Quoted in Westman, *op. cit.,* p. 9.
10. Carl G. Jung, ed., *Man and His Symbols* (Doubleday & Co., 1964), p. 96.
11. Maurice S. Friedman, *Martin Buber: The Life of Dialogue* (Harper & Brothers, 1960), p. 230.

Chapter VI. Image and Sign

1. Paul Tillich, *Systematic Theology,* Vol. II (The University of Chicago Press, 1957), p. 33.
2. Cassirer, *The Philosophy of Symbolic Forms,* Vol. II, p. 42.
3. Ladislas Segy, *African Sculpture Speaks* (A. A. Wyn, 1952), p. 100.
4. *Ibid.*
5. Erich Kahler, in Rollo May, ed., *Symbolism in Religion and Literature* (George Braziller, 1960), pp. 60 f.
6. Polanyi, *op. cit.,* p. 405.
7. *Ibid.*
8. Cassirer, *The Philosophy of Symbolic Forms,* Vol. II, p. 238.

9. In Lyman Bryson, *et al.*, eds., *Symbols and Society* (Harper & Brothers, 1955), p. 207.

10. *The Bridge*, Judeo-Christian Yearbook (Pantheon Press, 1962), p. 323.

11. Bryson, *et al.*, eds., *op. cit.*, pp. 405 f.

12. See *The Listener*, Aug. 9, 1962, p. 207.

13. Charles W. Morris, *Signs, Language and Behavior* (Prentice-Hall, Inc., 1946), Ch. 7.

14. Foss, *op. cit.*, p. 146.

15. Polanyi, *op. cit.*, pp. 94 f.

16. Arnold J. Toynbee, "Symbols Men Live—and Die—For," *The New York Times Magazine*, Nov. 20, 1960, p. 13.

17. See Tillich, *Systematic Theology*, Vol. I (The University of Chicago Press, 1951), pp. 115 ff., 238 ff.

18. "Symbol," *Hastings Encyclopedia of Religion and Ethics*, Vol. XII, 1922 ed., p. 139.

Chapter VII. The Productive Imagination

1. Th. Ribot, *Essay on the Creative Imagination* (London: Kegan Paul, Trench, Trubner & Co., 1906), p. 332.

2. Susanne Langer, *Feeling and Form* (Charles Scribner's Sons, 1953), p. 189.

3. *Ibid.*, p. 190.

4. *The New York Times*, Dec. 31, 1961.

5. Quoted in Albert William Levi, *Literature, Philosophy, and the Imagination* (Indiana University Press, 1962), Ch. 3.

6. Quoted in E. H. Johnson, *The Religious Use of the Imagination* (Silver Burdett & Co., 1901), p. 40.

7. *Ibid.*

8. Cassirer, *The Philosophy of Symbolic Forms*, Vol. I, p. 19.

9. *Ibid.*

10. *The Saturday Evening Post*, Jan. 21, 1961.

11. See *The New York Times*, Sept. 18, 1960.

12. Quoted in *Craft Horizons*, Nov.–Dec., 1961, p. 35.

13. *Ibid.*

14. John Ruskin, *Ethics of the Dust* (London: George Allen, 1903), pp. 229 f.

15. Nicolas Berdyaev, *The Meaning of the Creative Act*

(Harper & Brothers, 1954), p. 243.

16. Quoted in Levi, *op. cit.*, Ch. 4.

17. Cassirer, *The Philosophy of Symbolic Forms,* Vol. III, p. 182.

18. Richard Kroner, *The Religious Function of Imagination* (Yale University Press, 1941), p. 24.

19. *Ibid.*, p. 29.

20. *Ibid.*, p. 41.

Chapter VIII. The Shaping Power of Symbolic Forms

1. Schilpp, ed., *op. cit.*, pp. 1–39.

2. Rainer Maria Rilke, *Rodin* (London: The Grey Walls Press, Ltd., 1946).

3. Cassirer, *The Logic of the Humanities,* p. 215.

4. Cassirer, *The Philosophy of Symbolic Forms,* Vol. I, p. 74.

5. *Ibid.*

6. *Ibid.*, p. 114.

7. *Ibid.*

8. See particularly *The Myth of the State.*

9. Cassirer, *An Essay on Man,* p. 275.

10. Cassirer, *The Logic of the Humanities,* p. 190.

11. Cassirer, *The Philosophy of Symbolic Forms,* Vol. I, pp. 86 f.

Chapter IX. Bridges to the Understanding of Modern Man: Art

1. Katharine Gilbert in Schilpp, ed., *op. cit.*, p. 609.

2. Ernst Cassirer, *Das Symbolproblem und seine Stellung im System der Philosophie,* quoted in Schilpp, ed., *op. cit.*, p. 609.

3. See Langer, *Feeling and Form,* p. 399.

4. Erich Neumann, *Art and the Creative Unconscious* (Pantheon Books, Bollingen Series LXI, 1959), p. 103.

5. In John W. Dixon, Jr., *Nature and Grace in Art* (University of North Carolina Press, 1964).

6. *Ibid.*, Ch. 3.

7. Karl Jaspers, *The Future of Mankind,* p. 288.

8. *Ibid.*, p. 287.

9. Westman, *op. cit.*, p. 38.

Chapter X. Emerging Patterns of New Vision

1. Roland Penrose, *Picasso: His Life and Work* (London: Victor Gollancz, 1958), Ch. X.

2. Mary Seth, "Monument to Peace," *Presbyterian Life*, Jan. 1, 1962, pp. 21 f.

3. Gilbert Cope, "Controversial Canterbury," *Protestant Church Building*, Nov., 1962, pp. 13 f.

4. Vera Russell and John Russell, "Moore Explains His 'Universal Shapes,'" *The New York Times Magazine*, Nov. 11, 1962, pp. 60 f.

5. Digby, *op. cit.*, p. 67.

6. *Ibid.*, p. 102.

7. Sommerville Story, *Rodin* (London: Phaidon Press, Ltd., 1964), p. 12.

8. Robert Brustein, *The Theatre of Revolt* (Atlantic Monthly Press; Little, Brown and Company, 1964).

9. Leonard C. Pronko, *The World of Jean Anouilh* (University of California Press, 1961), p. 130.

10. *Ibid.*

11. T. S. Eliot, *The Waste Land*, in *Collected Poems, 1909–1962* (Harcourt, Brace and World, Inc., 1963). Quotations are reprinted with permission of the publisher.

12. Maud Bodkin, *Archetypal Patterns in Poetry* (Vintage Books, 1958), p. 313.

13. Johannes Riedel, "Albert Schweitzer's Bach," *The Christian Century*, March 23, 1960, p. 349.

Chapter XI. Symbols of the Transcendent and the Secular

1. Bewkes, ed., *op. cit.*, Ch. 6 (Reinhold Niebuhr).

2. Amos N. Wilder, *The Language of the Gospel; Early Christian Rhetoric* (Harper & Row, Publishers, Inc., 1964), p. 19. (Quoted from Clemens Benda.)

3. Peter Selz, *New Images of Man* (Museum of Modern Art, New York, 1959).

4. See Jacob Bronowski, *Insight* (Harper & Row, Publishers, Inc., 1964).

5. Polanyi, *op. cit.*, p. 395.

6. Johnson, ed., *op. cit.*, p. 53. (In a chapter by Abraham J. Heschel.)

7. See Part I of Harvey Cox, *The Secular City* (The Macmillan Company, 1965).

8. Arend Th. Van Leeuwen, *Christianity in World History* (London: Edinburgh House Press, 1964).

9. See the report of a conference at Celigny, Switzerland, Sept. 5, 1959, on " The Meaning of the Secular."

10. William Temple, *Mens Creatrix* (The Macmillan Company, 1917), p. 126.

11. *Ibid.*, p. 127.

12. A. C. Bridge, *Images of God* (London: Hodder & Stoughton, Ltd., 1960), p. 134.